TWENTIETH CENTURY INTERPRETATIONS
OF
DOCTOR
FAUSTUS

A Collection of Critical Essays

Edited by
WILLARD FARNHAM

Prentice-Hall, Inc. Englewood Cliffs, N. J.

A SPECTRUM BOOK

Literary criticism

131162

Current printing (last number):

10 9 8 7 6 5 4 3 2 1

Prentice-Hall International, Inc. (*London*)

Contents

v

Introduction

by Willard Farnham

I

Marlowe's *Doctor Faustus* is in some ways inseparable from his *Tamburlaine*. The two plays come together in the contributions they make to a theme that has characteristic expression in the culture of our postclassical Western world. Behind them both is essentially the same vision of uncurbed striving on the part of a hero that leads him to become an enemy of God by engaging in a flight toward the infinite. Yet they show extraordinarily different levels of achievement in Marlowe. Despite the damaged state in which *Doctor Faustus* has reached us, we find true greatness in it and recognize that it foreshadows much of deepest consequence to us in poetry that was to come. Most notably it foreshadows Shakespeare's *Macbeth,* Milton's *Paradise Lost,* and Goethe's *Faust.* There is nothing comparable prefigured by *Tamburlaine.*

In all likelihood Marlowe began the writing of *Tamburlaine* even while he was a student at Cambridge, for it was put on the London stage almost as soon as he had left the university with an M.A. Apparently it was staged as early as 1587–88, the second part immediately after the first. It was a memorable success. Marlowe, 23 years old in 1587, and Shakespeare's senior by only about two months, became a man of mark in the London theater world well before Shakespeare. When he was stabbed to death in 1593 at an inn in Deptford by one Ingram Frizer, the circumstances of the affair together with the characters of Frizer and two other men present were such as to raise suspicion that his end came as the result of plotting and counterplotting in a dubious minor world of secret agency and government spying, which he seems to have entered while still at Cambridge. There is basis, part of it a record of his engaging in a sword-and-dagger street encounter that led to the killing of a man (though by another hand than his), for thinking of Marlowe as being ready to court death in the same spirit of excess he had made so fully his own in the plays. In that part of his short life which he could give to poetry, his course of major dramatic achievement runs, according to one view held by critics, from *Tamburlaine* through *Doctor Faustus* and *The Jew of Malta* to *Edward II*, or, according to another view, from *Tamburlaine* through *The Jew of Malta* and *Edward II* to *Doctor Faustus*.

Whether *Edward II* or *Doctor Faustus* is Marlowe's last play is still an open question. But *Doctor Faustus* is now more often thought to be his last play than it was at the beginning of the twentieth century, partly because of a carefully reasoned bibliographical argument offered by W. W. Greg.[1]

Along with a growing inclination to see *Doctor Faustus* as Marlowe's last play goes a pronounced increase of esteem for it and a tendency to appraise it as showing a Marlowe much more mature than the Marlowe of *Tamburlaine*. There was a tendency in the latter part of the nineteenth century and the early part of the twentieth to consider that Marlowe reached maturity in *Edward II* with a realistic character study such as had come to be especially valued in the nineteenth century. Havelock Ellis is speaking as a representative of his time in the essay introductory to his Mermaid edition of Marlowe's major plays when he says that in *Edward II* "passionate poetry is subdued with severe self-restraint in a supreme tragic creation" and that here, finally, "Marlowe reached the summit of his art." [2] In our own time Dame Helen Gardner can begin a discussion of *Doctor Faustus* (which is reprinted in the present collection of interpretations) by calling it with all confidence Marlowe's greatest play though a much mutilated one. And when maturity is the consideration, John D. Jump in his Revels Plays edition of *Doctor Faustus* can say that "readers who find a remarkable emotional maturity in the best scenes of *Doctor Faustus* may reasonably hesitate to ascribe it to a date too close to that of *Tamburlaine*." [3] This judicious editor thinks that, with more objective arguments also taken into account, "the case for the later date [the last year of Marlowe's life] remains the stronger." [4]

In both *Tamburlaine* and *Doctor Faustus* the hero strives against human limitations conceived in the medieval Christian tradition. In *Tamburlaine* he defies Fortune and dares her to show the fickleness she is in duty bound to show. As a conqueror of kingdoms he climbs from peak to peak of success and never knows failure. He never joins those princes who, by falling from heights of prosperity to depths of misfortune in the manner of medieval tragedy, become edifying re-minders that the world of material rewards can never be dominated

---

[1] See the Introduction to W. W. Greg, ed., *Marlowe's Doctor Faustus, 1604–1616: Parallel Texts* (Oxford: Clarendon Press, 1950), pp. 1–14.

[2] Havelock Ellis, ed., *Christopher Marlowe* (London: T. Fisher Unwin; New York: Charles Scribner's Sons, n.d. [1893]), p. xlii.

[3] John D. Jump, ed., *Doctor Faustus* (London: Methuen & Co. Ltd., 1962, reprinted 1965), p. xxv.

[4] *Ibid.*, p. xxvi.

by man, and that indeed this world should be religiously contemned. Tamburlaine fears God no more than Fortune. He even forces himself upon God as an ally when he counts himself as "the scourge of God" in putting down enemies. Just as Marlowe himself later in his life was accused of atheism for allegedly not being God-fearing in accepted ways, so the hero of his first play was called, by Robert Greene as early as 1588, "that Atheist *Tamburlan*" for temerity shown in "daring God out of heaven." [5] Tamburlaine reduces to nothing the traditional limitation of mortal man imaged in the "strumpet Fortune," allowed by God to create the vicissitudes of worldly action by turning her wheel capriciously. To use words of Shakespeare's given the Player who declaims for Hamlet an account of the burning of Troy and the slaughter of Priam (with every appearance of mocking Marlowe's Tamburlainean style), Marlowe has Tamburlaine do to Fortune what the Player calls upon the gods to do. He has him

> Break all the spokes and fellies from her wheel,
> And bowl the round nave down the hill of heaven,
> As low as to the fiends.
>
> *(Hamlet,* II, ii, 517–19)

It is a Marlowe delighting in the subversion of a religious convention who is thus at work.

But even as he glorifies the "atheist" Tamburlaine Marlowe can put a part of religious convention to dramatic use without subverting it, particularly at the end of the drama. Tamburlaine in his long career as conqueror of kingdoms may defy Fortune with impunity, the Fortune who makes worldly conquerers fall from her wheel and who by doing so in religious representations offers men the reminder that heaven and not the mutable earthly scene is their true home. But there comes a time when he encounters Death. Him he cannot defy with impunity, the Death who in the Christian tradition leads the Dance of Death and offers much the same reminder offered by Fortune. As Tamburlaine comes to realize that he is dying, he cries out in his conqueror's vein to demand "what daring god" torments his body thus. When he actually sees "the ugly monster Death" before him, he claims mastery over him as having made him his "slave" by forcing him to devour so many of his enemies. But the monster will not be put off, and Tamburlaine, the would-be conqueror of all on earth, finally grants that it is Death who must be recognized as "the monarch of the earth." Moreover, when he yields to Death, he finds that Death

---

[5] Robert Greene, *Perimides the Blacksmith,* "epistle to the gentlemen readers," sig. A3; *The Life and Complete Works in Prose and Verse of Robert Greene,* ed. Alexander B. Grosart (London: privately circulated, 1881–86; New York: Russell and Russell, 1964), VII, p. 8.

has the power to make him look toward a life beyond his life on earth, somewhat as the figure of Death in a Dance of Death would be meant to do. With his dead queen placed by his side, his beloved Zenocrite, whose body he has preserved in a sheathing of gold, he grows confident of a coming opportunity to see her with spiritual eyes. His eyes will "glut" their "longings with a heaven of joy." There is thus to be a Tamburlainean Elysium, however different from a Christian heaven this may prove. But little is said of it, and what is said comes only at the play's end.

II

In *Doctor Faustus* Marlowe puts religious convention that is indubitably Christian so fully to dramatic use and is so far from subverting any part of it in Tamburlainean fashion that the result can only be called amazing if he wrote the play immediately after *Tamburlaine*. It is striking in any case. Faustus strives against human limitation to the point of selling his soul wittingly. This is not something that Tamburlaine is capable of doing. Marlowe makes Faustus a knower and a desirer to know as well as a seeker for power; Tamburlaine he does not.

Human limitation takes a form in *Doctor Faustus* as different from that in *Tamburlaine* as Faustus himself is different from the hero of the earlier play. Essentially the limitation in *Tamburlaine* is one that is outside man and the limitation in *Doctor Faustus* one that is inside him. Tamburlaine strives against a scheme of things in his surrounding world. This scheme contains men who fight to keep from being conquered and ruled, a Fortune who overthrows conquerors along with other ambitious climbers, and a Death who ends the lives of conquerors as well as of other men. But Faustus strives against a scheme of things implanted within his consciousness. It is a scheme of good and evil as opposites. It is the scheme that man finds within himself as soon as he eats of the tree of knowledge of good and evil and comes to know evil as that which for him insists upon being the not-good. Faustus reaches a point where, knowing evil with certainty, he refuses to be barred by recognition of it from attempting to make a part of it into his good as he strives to explore life infinitely.

What Marlowe creates out of the story of Faustus is a medieval morality play with a late Renaissance temper. Its Renaissance temper is, however, not immediately apparent. The play seems at first a curiously faithful revival of religious drama from an unsophisticated older age by the playwright least likely in his time to do such reviving. It has a figure of humanity who embraces evil-doing and imperils his soul. He is led by figures of evil deeper and deeper into peril, becomes corrupted with worldly delights, and, when he feels despair, considers committing suicide. Yet he finds himself fought for by opposing figures of good and is reminded that divine mercy is always available to him if he repents. Since he does not avail himself of this mercy, he is doomed to suffer damnation in hell. All this is familiar in the later morality play, where the failure of mercy to prevail became possible and brought about tragical endings not to be found in the earlier morality play. Yet *Doctor Faustus* is not rightly to be taken as evidence of a thorough change of spirit in Marlowe.

From the very beginning Marlowe's Faustus is too much a stiff-necked pursuer of his own way to be all that he should be as a figure of man in a medieval morality play. We do not see a typical morality-play temptation by a figure of evil, whether man or devil, prevailing upon an innocent Faustus to start him upon a course of evil-doing. We see a knowing Faustus deliberately setting himself upon an evil course. He is a scholar overpowered by his intellectual pride, "swollen with cunning of a self-conceit," as the Chorus says in the Prologue. The Chorus presents one aspect of his tragedy in two lines:

> His waxen wings did mount above his reach,
> And, melting, heavens conspir'd his overthrow.
> (Prologue, 21–22)[6]

Thus Marlowe, when he introduces Faustus, makes him a challenger of heaven as a soaring Icarus. But speaking also in other than classical terms, he makes him a man bent upon adding to the Icarian challenge that of the "devilish exercise" of magic. The magic is "cursed." Nevertheless, Faustus prefers it "before his chiefest bliss."

Immediately after the action begins, when Faustus has decided to reach beyond all that he has learned in the study of philosophy, medicine, law, and divinity and to undertake the study of magic, he is visited by his friends Valdes and Cornelius. He says that by what they have told him about magic they have helped him make his decision. But he will not have it that they did more than encourage him to follow a path of thought that was his own. Their words had effect, he grants, and then adds:

[6] My quotations from *Doctor Faustus* are from the edition of John D. Jump, previously cited. This edition numbers scenes and lines within scenes without making act divisions. Where I refer to a scene by Jump's numbering I also give a corresponding reference to act and scene with the line numbering that Boas and Greg have brought into use in their editions. Some of the authors whose comments on the play are reprinted in the present collection give references by continuous line numbering in the manner used by Tucker Brooke in his edition of Marlowe's *Works* (Oxford: Clarendon Press, 1910).

> Yet not your words only, but mine own fantasy,
> That will receive no object, for my head
> But ruminates on necromantic skill.
>
> (i—or I, i—100–102)

In short, he really does not need a tempter. Valdes recognizes in Faustus
something that might be called predilection combined with genius for
the kind of evil to be undertaken. In answer to the request made by
Faustus for "some demonstrations magical," Valdes agrees to become
his instructor, but in a way strangely deferential:

> First I'll instruct thee in the rudiments,
> And then wilt thou be perfecter than I.
>
> (i—160–61)

Nor does Mephostophilis first appear to Faustus as a devil who walks
up and down in the earth to tempt and corrupt any man encountered.
He appears because he senses in Faustus' magical summons that Faustus is already corrupt, that indeed he is already "in danger to be
damned."

When it comes to the agreement with Mephostophilis by which
Faustus gains magical power, it is clear, however, that Marlowe holds
his hero back from what, according to at least one Christian view,
would be a complete giving of himself to evil. He does not let him go
so far as the Faustus who is the subject of the anonymous *Historia
von D. Iohañ Fausten* published in Germany in 1587, which is obviously the work of a Lutheran. An English translation of this *Faust-
buch*, made by an unknown with the initials P. F. and entitled *The
Historie of the Damnable Life and Deserved Death of Doctor Iohn
Faustus*, was published in 1592 with indication on the title-page that
the edition was not the first ("newly imprinted, and in convenient
places imperfect matter amended"). Marlowe often follows the English
version of the *Historia* closely, and up to a point follows closely what
is given there about the articles of agreement between Faustus and
Mephostophilis. After that point he omits certain articles of agreement entirely.

Marlowe's Faustus makes five conditions that Mephostophilis promises to fulfill. They begin with the stipulation that he, Faustus, may be
a "spirit in form and substance" (i.e., have the spiritual power of a
devil), and they proceed with stipulations as to ways in which Mephostophilis shall serve him and be at his command. In the *Damnable
Life* there are the same five conditions in the same order, and they
have almost exactly the same wording. What Marlowe's Faustus agrees
to in exchange is the surrender of all that constitutes himself: "body
and soul, flesh, blood, or goods," which at the end of 24 years Lucifer

and Mephostophilis may carry "into their habitation wheresoever."
The legalistic array of words for that which is given is exactly the same
in the *Damnable Life*.

But in the *Damnable Life* something more is agreed to by Faustus.
He will at once become an enemy of Christianity and Christians and,
indeed, of all creation. He will defy God and his Christ and all the
host of heaven. More than that, he will set himself not only against all
creatures made in the shape of God but even against all that live. In
other words, he will join the army of evil and, ranging himself with the
devils, will oppose not only God but likewise all God's handiwork.

Near the end of the *Damnable Life,* when Faustus says farewell to
his fellow scholars just before he is carried off to hell, he tells them
that he actually has been thus inimical to God and man. Marlowe in
his corresponding scene (xix—or V, ii) offers a very different Faustus.
In bidding farewell to his fellows Marlowe's Faustus tells them that he
has "abjured" and "blasphemed" God, but he says nothing of having
been an enemy of mankind and all else that lives. Yet he implies that
he has been an enemy of one man, himself. For he has cut himself off
from a God who, he is convinced, would have shown him mercy in
answer to a petition for it. He has sold his soul, and it has gradually
become so much enslaved that at last it cannot move him to ask God's
forgiveness. He can be controlled now from within as well as from
without by infernal power. "Ah, my God," he cries, "I would weep but
the devil draws in my tears. . . . O, he stays my tongue! I would lift
up my hands, but see, they hold them, they hold them." Possessed
spiritually in this way, he finds it is "now too late" to win mercy.
There is no such subtle possession of Faustus in the *Damnable Life,*
though he is terrorized into subjection, as he is also in *Doctor Faustus.*

An outstanding instance of terrorization in *Doctor Faustus* is that
following the struggle between the Good Angel and the Bad Angel
which the Good Angel wins to the extent of getting Faustus to call out,

> O Christ, my saviour, my saviour,
> Help to save distressed Faustus' soul.
> (vi—or II, ii—85–86)

The devils immediately sense the threat of loss, and a trio of them
appear—Lucifer himself, Beelzebub, and Mephostophilis. Faustus is
overcome with terror. He is convinced that he is to be claimed before
the time agreed upon. Abjectly he promises:

> Never to name God or to pray to him,
> To burn his scriptures, slay his ministers,
> And make my spirits pull his churches down.

Here then, under duress, Faustus promises to be an enemy of Christianity. But even so he does not promise to be an enemy of his fellow men and the rest of God's living creation.[7] The promise he does make is merely a desperate placation of the devils. It does not show in his own actions later.

III

Doctor Faustus is an extension of the traditional morality drama in which the figure Mankind is a very different protagonist from that which he once was. He does not now appear at the beginning of the action as a poor innocent who is totally ignorant of the ways of the world, the flesh, and the devil that he is called upon to resist. In the person of Faustus he comes knowing much about these three, but unaware that his knowledge is by no means all that is necessary. In the pride of his learning he is confident that he can bargain to his own advantage with the devil for gratifications of the world and the flesh.

The learning of Faustus has brought him to think that Christianity cramps man's striving. But nevertheless, in ways already discussed, he shows himself not disposed to work destruction upon Christianity or to be malicious toward his fellow men, whom Christianity would urge him to love. He is simply casting aside what he calls the "old wives' tales" of religion in order that he may here and now, in the only life of which he is sure, live more fully. Christianity speaks of hell for those who cast it aside. But, says he to Mephostophilis as he delivers to him the agreement to surrender his soul at the end of 24 years, "I think hell's a fable." "Ay," says Mephostophilis, no longer fearing to lose his prey and speaking from the midst of the eternal hell that he carries about with him wherever he goes, "think so still, till experience change thy mind."

The rest of the drama brings mind-changing experience to Faustus. He discovers that the "fable" of hell contains unsuspected layers of truth. For soon after he has deeded away his soul, he enters an ever-present private hell like that of Mephostophilis, and into it he sinks deeper and deeper. Though he has bargained to have powerful spirits obey his every command, he is quickly conscious that, instead of en-slaving these spirits, he has been enslaved by them. He cannot hide his thoughts and actions from them, whereas they can hide theirs from him. He cannot have doubts about whether he has made a good bargain without their knowing of them and, if things get to a certain

---

[7] These three lines, found in the A-text (1604) of the play, are not in the B-text (1616). A question can be raised whether they are Marlowe's. But it seems that they are, for reasons given by Greg, *op. cit.*, p. 85 and note to A 726–28, pp. 339–40.

point of seriousness, without their taking steps to stop him from thinking and acting. He is literally bedeviled by them.

Awareness comes to Faustus that he has already lost his soul long before the death that he must meet at the end of the specified 24 years. Not only has his soul been captured by powers that do not wish it well, but even before its capture it had been lost in the sense that it had strayed and made itself ready to be stolen in its pursuit of magic. He has deserted an arduous path leading to new knowledge and sought for quick and easy gains. In his boundless desire to go forward, he has actually turned backward. His fascination with magic would not have seemed strange to Marlowe's audience. Marlowe lived in an age when a fair number of well-endowed minds were giving consideration to the ancient symbolism of magic as possibly having new virtue for the human race. An era had begun in which man's control of nature was to be greatly extended by what is now known as scientific method, but to these minds it seemed that an extension which was obviously destined might logically come about through application of a magical method. They thought that an old picture of the universe as animated in all its parts was one to which man in his quest for new capability should give attention. If man could, by knowledge of processes that bind, control the spirits essential to nature, including the spirits within the four elements of earth, water, air, and fire, he would in the most direct way be master of the world around him. As C. S. Lewis well says, in a discussion of the new learning of the Renaissance, the new magic had no small place among dreams of power. It had a place beside the thought of Bacon, though we of the present cannot easily see why, "because we know that science succeeded and magic failed." [8]

There had been condemnation of magic from the early days of Christianity, although magic in the Renaissance did not lack avowedly Christian defenders. Any attempt to deal with spirits, even with those in the four elements, could of course be condemned on religious grounds. Devils inherited by Christianity from Judaism were often associated in various ways with the nature spirits of a lore not Biblical. The result was that there could be warning against such spirits as well as against spirits from hell, and, indeed, nature spirits were sometimes thought of as being in the dominion of Lucifer. When Faustus conjures to summon Mephostophilis, he begins by spurning the threefold spirit of Jehovah (the Trinity), then hails the spirits of fire, air, water, and earth, and then asks the favor of Lucifer, Beelzebub, and Demogorgon that Mephostophilis may appear.

Marlowe gives to Faustus a dream of power similar to but more

[8] C. S. Lewis, *English Literature in the Sixteenth Century Excluding Drama* (Oxford: Clarendon Press, 1954), p. 13.

subtle in design of action than Tamburlaine's. It is again a conqueror's dream, but one in which dominance is to be attained by finesse of knowledge instead of main strength. Faustus is a scholar and, as he turns to magic as a way to infinite power, he has an urge to take the pursuit of knowledge also into the infinite. However, he is never concerned with carrying on the pursuit of "pure" knowledge—knowledge for its own sake or for the advancement of human comprehension. His longing is for the knowledge that, as we now say, can be "applied," not the knowledge to which poets and prophets contribute. From the very beginning his dream has about it something of the rankness of Tamburlaine's. It looks forward to "profit and delight" and to "honour" gained by "omnipotence." It even looks forward to a Faustus who will be "great emperor of the world," just as Tamburlaine's dream looks forward to a Tamburlaine who will be "general of the world."

But the dramas of Tamburlaine and Faustus as dreamers of power are utterly different in the shaping Marlowe gives them. Tamburlaine all but becomes general of the world, meeting no check in his conquering until he dies a natural death in advanced years. Faustus, on the contrary, falls so far short of becoming emperor of the world that he never once begins to conquer kingdoms and even loses the empery of himself after meeting check after check to his confidence and being haunted by the thought of the terrifying death he has arranged for as part of his self-surrender. The height of his achievement is possession of Trojan Helen as his paramour. Yet even she can be no more for him than a conjured-up simulacrum.

Doctor Faustus is thus the tragedy of a man who in striving boundlessly misdirects great gifts of mind and spirit and hence progressively loses his soul by disintegration as well as by capture. Progressive disintegration in Faustus brings low comedy into the tragedy, to echo clownishly what he is doing to himself or even to draw him into its clownishness. Much of this is far from having the verve and the dramatic import characteristic of Shakespearean low comedy. It has often been held, and not only because of a desire to protect the reputation of Marlowe, that some at least of the comic scenes are not his work. When Faustus himself turns comedian, one may have the thought that Marlowe is making low comedy show the tragic failure of his hero to live up to his high hopes of benefit from magic—a failure that brings him to playing jejune tricks on the world instead of taking imperial control of it or even transforming it. But, the textual problems raised by the play being what they are, one cannot be sure that some or all of the magical tricks he plays were not contributed to the action by someone other than Marlowe who was intent only upon amusing his audience in the most obvious and easy way. There is much variation, even much variation in length, between the two texts of the play from which a modern editor has to work, the A-text (1604 and later editions) and the B-text (1616 and later editions); and Greg, after his intensive examination of these, is moved to add his own voice to what he rightly calls a "general agreement among editors and critics" that neither text "can be ascribed to Marlowe as a whole." [9] It is indicated, however, that Marlowe planned the play ("grandly," as Goethe said) and that his hand is strongly in control at its beginning and its end.

The comment of the Chorus at the end of *Doctor Faustus* is in part the moral of a morality play. In terms of the Christian tradition in which the play is mainly cast it offers an orthodox warning. Faustus has done what "heavenly power" does not permit. He has suffered damnation. "Forward wits" should take heed.

But in part this choral comment also does something very different. In its well-known first three lines it offers a view of the tragedy, rather than the morality drama, of Faustus. It puts the tragedy in terms of a tradition other than the Christian:

> Cut is the branch that might have grown full straight,
> And burned is Apollo's laurel bough
> That sometime grew within this learned man.
>
> (Epilogue, 1–3)

There is good reason to think that all of the concluding comment assigned to the Chorus is Marlowe's, but these three lines assuredly bear his poetic signature. Though they evoke no divinity of Sinai who forbids, but a divinity of Olympus who inspires, they make it plain that any complete refusal by a man to cherish a gift of Apollonian laurel implanted within him and any resultant seeking for magical ease of achievement must mean an ending in the fires of Gehenna. The God in *Doctor Faustus* is not mocked with any less peril when he inspires than when he forbids.

[9] Greg, *op. cit.*, p. 97.

The Rehabilitation of Faustus

by George Santayana

An adventurer in the romantic as well as in the vulgar sense of the word, somewhat like Paracelsus or Giordano Bruno, Doctor Faustus had felt the mystery of nature, had scorned authority, had credited magic, had lived by imposture, and had fled from the police. His blasphemous boasts and rascally conduct, together with his magic arts, had made him even in his lifetime a scandalous and interesting personage. He was scarcely dead when legends gathered about his name. It was published abroad that he had sold his soul to the devil, in exchange for twenty-four years of wild pleasures upon earth.

This legend purported to offer a terrible and edifying example, a warning to all Christians to avoid the snares of science, of pleasure, and of ambition. These things had sent Doctor Faustus into hell-fire; his corpse, found face downward, could not be turned over upon its back. Nevertheless, we may suspect that even at the beginning people recognized in Doctor Faustus a braver brother, a somewhat enviable reprobate who had dared to relish the good things of this life above the sad joys vaguely promised for the other. All that the Renaissance valued was here represented as in the devil's gift; and the man in the street might well doubt whether it was religion or worldly life that was thereby made the more unlovely. Doubtless the Lutheran authors of the first chapbook felt, and felt rightly, that those fine things which tempted Faustus were unevangelical, pagan, and popish; yet they could not cease altogether to admire and even to covet them, especially when the first ardours of the Old-Christian revival had had time to cool.

Marlowe, who wrote only a few years later, made a beginning in the rehabilitation of the hero. His Faustus is still damned, but he is transformed into the sort of personage that Aristotle approves of for the hero of tragedy, essentially human and noble, but led astray by some

"*The Rehabilitation of Faustus*" (*Editor's title*). *From* Three Philosophical Poets: Lucretius, Dante, and Goethe *by George Santayana* (*Cambridge, Massachusetts: Harvard University Press, 1910*), *pp. 145-53. Copyright, 1910, by Harvard University Press, 1938 by George Santayana. Reprinted by permission of the publisher.*

excusable vice or error. Marlowe's public would see in Doctor Faustus a man and a Christian like themselves, carried a bit too far by ambition and the love of pleasure. He is no radical unbeliever, no natural mate for the devil, conscienceless and heathen, like the typical villain of the Renaissance. On the contrary, he has become a good Protestant, and holds manfully to all those parts of the creed which express his spontaneous affections. A good angel is often overheard whispering in his ear; and if the bad angel finally prevails, it is in spite of continual remorse and hesitation on the Doctor's part. This excellent Faustus is damned by accident or by predestination; he is brow-beaten by the devil and forbidden to repent when he has really repented. The terror of the conclusion is thereby heightened; we see an essentially good man, because in a moment of infatuation he had signed away his soul, driven against his will to despair and damnation. The alternative of a happy solution lies almost at hand; and it is only a lingering taste for the lurid and the horrible, ingrained in this sort of melodrama, that sends him shrieking to hell.

What makes Marlowe's conclusion the more violent and the more unphilosophical is the fact that, to any one not dominated by convention, the good angel, in the dialogue, seems to have so much the worse of the argument. All he has to offer is sour admonition and external warnings:

> *O Faustus, lay that damnèd book aside,*
> *And gaze not on it lest it tempt thy soul,*
> *And heap God's heavy wrath upon thy head.*
> *Read, read, the Scriptures; that is blasphemy. . . .*
> *Sweet Faustus, think of heaven, and heavenly things.*

To which the evil angel replies:

> *No, Faustus, think of honour and of wealth.*

And in another place:

> *Go forward, Faustus, in that famous art,*
> *Wherein all nature's treasure is contained.*
> *Be thou on earth as Jove is in the sky,*
> *Lord and commander of these elements.*

There can be no doubt that the devil here represents the natural ideal of Faustus, or of any child of the Renaissance; he appeals to the vague but healthy ambitions of a young soul, that would make trial of the world. In other words, this devil represents the true good, and it is no wonder if the honest Faustus cannot resist his suggestions. We like him for his love of life, for his trust in nature, for his enthusiasm for beauty. He speaks for us all when he cries:

Was this the face that launched a thousand ships
And burnt the topless towers of Ilium?

Even his irreverent pranks, being directed against the pope, endear him the more to an anti-clerical public; and he appeals to courtiers and cavaliers by his lofty poetical scorn for such crabbed professions as the law, medicine, or theology. In a word, Marlowe's Faustus is a martyr to everything that the Renaissance prized,—power, curious knowledge, enterprise, wealth, and beauty.

How thoroughly Marlowe and Goethe are on the way towards reversing the Christian philosophy of life may be seen if we compare *Faust* for a moment (as, in other respects, has often been done) with *The Wonder-working Magician* of Calderon. This earlier hero, St. Cyprian of Antioch, is like Faust in being a scholar, signing away his soul to the devil, practising magic, embracing the ghost of beauty, and being ultimately saved. Here the analogy ends. Cyprian, far from being disgusted with all theory, and particularly with theology, is a pagan philosopher eagerly seeking God, and working his way, with full faith in his method, toward Christian orthodoxy. He floors the devil in scholastic argument about the unity of God, his power, wisdom, and goodness. He falls in love, and sells his soul merely in the hope of satisfying his passion. He studies magic chiefly for the same reason; but magic cannot overrule the free-will of the Christian lady he loves (a modern and very Spanish one, though supposed to adorn ancient Antioch). The devil can supply only a false phantasm of her person, and as Cyprian approaches her and lifts her veil, he finds a hideous death's-head beneath; for God can work miracles to cap those of any magician, and can beat the devil at his own game. Thunderstruck at this portent, Cyprian becomes a Christian. Half-naked, ecstatic, taken for a madman, he bears witness loudly and persistently to the power, wisdom, and goodness of the one true God; and, since the persecution of Decius is then going on, he is hurried away to martyrdom. His lady, sentenced also for the same cause, encourages him by her heroic attitude and words. Their earthly passion is dead; but their souls are united in death and in immortality.

In this drama we see magic checkmated by miracles, doubt yielding to faith, purity resisting temptation, passion transformed into zeal, and all the glories of the world collapsing before disillusion and asceticism. These glories are nothing, the poet tells us, but dust, ashes, smoke, and air.

The contrast with Goethe's *Faust* could not be more complete. Both poets take the greatest liberties with their chronology, yet the spirit of their dramas is remarkably true to the respective ages in which they are supposed to occur. Calderon glorifies the movement from paganism to Christianity. The philosophy in which that movement culminated —Catholic orthodoxy—still dominates the poet's mind, not in a perfunctory way, but so as to kindle his imagination, and render his personages sublime and his verses rapturous. Goethe's *Faust,* on the contrary, glorifies the return from Christianity to paganism. It shows the spirit of the Renaissance liberating the soul, and bursting the bonds of traditional faith and traditional morals. This spirit, after manifesting itself brilliantly at the time of the historical Faust, had seemed to be smothered in the great world during the seventeenth century. Men's characters and laws had reaffirmed their old allegiance to Christianity, and the Renaissance survived only abstractly, in scholarship or the fine arts, to which it continued to lend a certain classic or pseudo-classic elegance. In Goethe's time, however, a second Renaissance was taking place in the souls of men. The love of life, primal and adventurous, was gathering head in many an individual. In the romantic movement and in the French Revolution, this love of life freed itself from the politic compromises and conventions that had been stifling it for two hundred years. Goethe's hero embodies this second, romantic emancipation of the mind, too long an unwilling pupil of Christian tradition. He cries for air, for nature, for all experience. Cyprian, on the other hand, an unwilling pupil of paganism, had yearned for truth, for solitude, and for heaven.

Such was the legend that, to the great good fortune of mankind, fascinated the young Goethe, and took root in his fancy. Around it gathered the experiences and insights of sixty well-filled years: *Faust* became the poetical autobiography and the philosophic testament of Goethe. He stuffed it with every enthusiasm that diversified his own life, from the great alternative of romantic or classical art, down to the controversy between Neptunism and Vulcanism in geology, and to his fatherly admiration for Lord Byron. Yet in spite of the liberties he took with the legend, and the personal turn he gave it, nothing in its historical associations escaped him. His life in Frankfort and in Strassburg had made the mediaeval scene familiar to his fancy; Herder had communicated to him an imaginative cult for all that was national and characteristic in art and manners; the spell of Gothic architecture had fallen on him; and he had learned to feel in Shakespeare the infinite strength of suggestion in details, in multitudinous glimpses, in lifelike medleys of sadness and mirth, in a humble realism in externals, amid lyric and metaphysical outpourings of the passions. The sense for classic beauty which had inspired Marlowe with immortal lines, and was later to inspire his own *Helena,* was as yet dormant; but instead he had caught the humanitarian craze, then prevalent, for defending and idealizing the victims of law and society, among others, the poor girl who, to escape disgrace, did away with her new-born child. Such a victim of a selfish seducer and a Pharisaical public was to add a desirable touch of femininity and pathos to the story of Faust: Gretchen was to take the place, at least for the nonce, of the coveted Helen.

Marlowe's *Faustus*

by M. C. Bradbrook

Faustus is comparatively domestic and familiar in its setting. The University of Wittenberg is thought of in terms of Cambridge: Faustus' relations with his scholars are quite different from Tamburlaine's with the kings: the conjurors Valdes and Cornelius are invited in to dinner (1. 1. 164–5) and the clowns are fully drawn yokels. All this makes the play more naturalistic, in spite of the supernatural element, as befits the more relaxed and colloquial verse.

The Prologue makes the transition from the stately stories of "proud audacious deeds" to "the form of Faustus' fortunes, good or bad." The very use of such a folk-legend suggests that Marlowe was no longer so scornful of popular taste, and the large provisions for spectacle cannot be wholly attributed to collaborators.

Yet the story itself required some conventional handling. It was more difficult to telescope Faustus' history than Tamburlaine's, and to give a panoramic view of the twenty-four years. It was also hard to get the objective correlative for Faustus' aspiring mind, when Marlowe had come down to particulars; he only succeeded in suggesting a worthy bribe in the figure of Helen.

Finally there was the comic relief. A recollection of Mycetes and an anticipation of *The Jew of Malta* will confirm the opinion of Dr. Boas that part of the comedy in *Faustus* is Marlowe's work and represents an attempt to give a burlesque subplot. The play is primarily a study of the mind of Faustus himself; his biography is arranged to show his mental development, rather than simply to present "the form of Faustus' fortunes, good or bad." For instance, the first speech of Faustus is, I think, meant to suggest in a telescoped fashion a long period of mental debate, not to represent a single occasion. The tempo is quickened beyond that of ordinary life, just as movements are speeded up sometimes in the cinema. The prologue, with its subtle

"Marlowe's Faustus" *(Editor's title). From* Themes and Conventions of Elizabethan Tragedy *by M. C. Bradbrook (Cambridge: Cambridge University Press, 1935), pp. 148–55. Copyright 1935 by the Syndics of the Cambridge University Press. Reprinted by permission of the publisher.*

and, I think, intentional confusion of tenses, prepares the spectator for a further summary presented in the form of a soliloquy.

> He *profits* in divinity. . . .
> His waxen wings *did mount* above his reach. . . .
> He *surfeits* upon cursed necromancy.   (Prologue)

Faustus, turning from one book to the next, represents in conventionalised form his own mental history, as the prologue has given the outward events of his life. (The good and bad angels are also, I think, not tutelary spirits but projections of Faustus' own contrary impulses.) In the first speeches, the mood of Tamburlaine is sometimes recalled.

> I'll have them fly to India for gold
> Ransack the ocean for orient pearl
> And search all corners of the new found world
> For pleasant fruits and princely delicates.
>
> (1. 1. 83ff.)

But this kind of exaltation does not last: Faustus descends to "the seignory of Embden" and silk gowns for his students. The drama might have been a simple extension of the conquering power of the Scythian:

> Emperors and kings
> Are but obeyed in their several provinces
> Nor can they raise the wind or rend the clouds,
> But his dominion that exceeds in this
> Stretcheth as far as doth the mind of man—
>
> (1. 1. 58ff.)

but as a matter of fact Faustus' ambition falls below Tamburlaine's; and his power, if greater in extent, is more shadowy. For even in the midst of his triumphs, he "is but Faustus and a man."

His character is in fact not one of fixed determination, as is so often asserted; he constantly wavers, and his purposes change. Sometimes he sounds immovable:

> This night I'll conjure, though I die therefore. . . .
>
> (1. 1. 167)
>
> Had I as many souls as there be stars,
> I'd give them all for Mephistopheles. . . .
>
> (1. 3. 104-5)

Yet he has continually to screw up his courage, as Macbeth has. Before he begins the conjuring, he says, half apprehensively:

> Then fear not, Faustus, to be resolute—

and his soliloquy at the opening of Act 2 is full of the twists and
doublings of his mind.

> Now, Faustus, must
> Thou needs be damned and canst thou not be saved
> What boots it then to think on God or heaven?
> Away with such vain fancies and despair.
> Despair in God and trust in Belzebub:
> Now go not backward: no, Faustus, be resolute.
>
> (2. 1. 1ff.)

If it takes so many negatives to stop Faustus' repentance there must be
very strong forces working for it. It is after this debate with himself
that the two angels again appear, as incarnations of the alternatives
before him. In this speech for the first time (and it is even before the
contract is signed) Faustus tells himself to "despair." The idea of
despair in the theological sense (that is, a conviction of damnation
such as the one from which John Bunyan suffered) runs through the
play. It is the means by which the devils, from the very beginning,
secure Faustus' soul, making him incapable of repentance, even though
he wills with all his might to repent. "Distressed" is also used as an
alternative description of this mental state. At other times, however,
Faustus is determined to an extent that makes his resolution appear
ludicrous. He can say to the devil himself:

> Learn thou of Faustus' manly fortitude
> And scorn those joys thou never shalt possess.
>
> (1. 3. 87–8)

His intoxication at his power to command the devil occasionally blinds
him to everything else, and when Mephistopheles tells him truthfully
of hell (2. 1. 116–40) he simply refuses to face it—

> I think hell's a fable.

Faustus' mind is revealed in the first two acts: it is seen swinging constantly between repentance and damnation, wavering remorse and
fixed pride. In 2. 2 there is a third repentance; the two angels again
appear symbolising the conflict, but their speeches are shorter and
sharper, and the passage ends with the triumph of the bad angel:

> Faustus never shall repent.   (2. 2. 17)

Immediately Faustus falls into "despair"—

> My heart is hardened, I cannot repent.   (2. 2. 18)

And he returns to his catechising of Mephistopheles; for this is the
means by which he salves his despair. At the end of this scene there is

the fourth and last conflict. Faustus goes further than before: he calls
upon Christ, and the devils come in to attack him. There is extraor-
dinary irony in the juxtaposition.

> *Faustus.* O Christ, my saviour, my saviour,
> Help to save distressed Faustus' soul!
>
> *Enter Lucifer, Belzebub and Mephistopheles.*   (2. 2. 85ff.)

This kind of irony of situation is paralleled by the use of quotations
with an ironic significance. Faustus, as he signs the bond, says "Consummatum est," the final words of Christ in St John's Gospel. It immediately reminds one of the masterly adaptation of Ovid:

> O lente, lente currite, noctis equi!

in the final soliloquy.

The middle part of the play contains nothing which could not be
spared, even if some of the writing is Marlowe's, except the few lines
before and after the horse courser's episode.

> Now Mephistopheles, the restless course
> That time does run with calm and silent foot
> Calls for the payment of my latest years: (4. 2*a*. 101ff.)

and

> What art thou Faustus but a man condemned to die? . . .
> Despair doth drive distrust into my thoughts . . .
> Tush, Christ did call the thief upon the cross
> Then rest thee, Faustus quiet in conceit.   (4. 5*a*. 29ff.)

The stealing away of time is hardly thought of in the bustle of
Faustus' conjuring, and the first speech brings up what is to be the
theme of the final soliloquy, the contrast of time and eternity; after
this it is impossible to forget the hour-glass. The second passage recalls
Faustus' earlier repentances and despairs, and his refusal to face the
consequences of his situation. But since Faustus' mind is meant to be
distracted with his pleasures during the four-and-twenty years, and
the tragedy is based on mental suffering, the interval could have little
significance for Marlowe.

In the last act the moods of the first two acts reappear. Faustus
repents (5. 1. 55ff.) and then he "despairs" and is about to commit
suicide; but his "distressed soul" is comforted by the old man. The
feeling cannot exist, however, without the support of the old man's
presence: as soon as he goes Faustus exclaims:

> I do repent: and yet I do despair.   (5. 1. 79)

Mephistopheles forces him to sign another bond; and Faustus drugs himself with Helen, whose embraces will extinguish "those thoughts which do dissuade me from my vows." The lovely invocation, though it is the most magnificent verse in the play, is quite cut off in style from the rest of it and is nearer to speeches of *Tamburlaine.*

The last scene begins in prose: it is simple, colloquial speech, stressing above all Faustus' humanity. His poignant feelings are shown through the repetition of phrases (compare the doubling of "lente" in the Ovidian line).

> What wonders I have done, all Germany can witness, yea, all the world: for which Faustus hath lost both Germany and the world: yea heaven itself, heaven the seat of God, the throne of the blessed, the kingdom of joy: and must remain in hell for ever—hell, ah, hell for ever! Sweet friends, what shall become of Faustus, being in hell for ever?

This repetition indicates Faustus' helplessness (he can only say the same thing over and over), and his fixation upon the single problem which at last he cannot evade. He already sounds broken: the devil's power over him is already of a physical kind, so that his despair is enforced: "I would lift up my hands—but see, they hold them, they hold them!" The repetition here has the effect of a plea; but whether mercy is asked of God or Mephistopheles does not emerge.

The scene which comes between the dialogue of the Scholars and the final soliloquy has been generally considered the addition of another hand. In any case, it offers the conventionalised version for the feeling which is poetically given in the soliloquy. The good and bad angels enter from opposite sides: heaven and the saints are disclosed to music: hell is revealed and described by the bad angel. It "exploits," as Dr Boas says, "the theatrical devices of the period." [1]

This scene is thoroughly based on the mediaeval stage, and whether Marlowe agreed to its presence or not, it suggests much about the temper of the play.

It acts as a spectacular prologue to the final soliloquy, rather as a dumb show might precede a play. The greatness of the final speech of Faustus depends not only on its poetic power, but the subtle way in which it gathers up and focusses all the feeling of the earlier scenes. For example:

> See, see where Christ's blood streams in the firmament,

[1] Introduction to the Methuen edition, p. 43. Though he seems to think the throne is a "state" or chair, and not the machine for descent from above. *Vide* Lawrence's article in *Pre-Restoration Stage Studies.* Also, it seems probable that hell was under the stage. It would not need to be described in such detail if, like the angels, it were visible. The trap might open, smoke and flames ascend, and Faustus look down into it. Cf. "Ugly hell, *gape not*" (5. 2. 193). There could not be one hell on a backcloth, as Dr Boas suggests, and another which "gaped."

besides being remodelled from *Tamburlaine,* suggests the scene where Faustus' own blood congealed, as he was about to sign the bond and he cried

> Why *streams* it not?

in his haste to sell his soul. His former moods reappear, intensified by the pressure of his feeling. He frantically denies the situation: tries to play King Canute as he had done for so long; to conjure in a more daring manner than ever.

> Stand still, you ever-moving spheres of heaven
> That time may cease and midnight never come;
> Fair Nature's eye, rise, rise again. . . .

The quick repetition comes because he is trying to cram as many words into his little hour as possible, and also, by repeating the same word, to give himself the illusion that time is not passing at all. He ends with desperate commands to body and soul, to God and the devils, as though by the exercise of his will he could reverse the course of events.

> Ugly hell, gape not! Come not, Lucifer!
> I'll burn my books—Ah, Mephistopheles.

The last is, of course, a scream (and so the reading proposed by Mr. Empson does not stand).[2]

[2] *Seven Types of Ambiguity,* p. 261.

Faustus as Allegory

by James Smith

The final scene in *Dr. Faustus* is more often than not treated as
irrelevant to the play. In it, says one critic, "Marlowe committed
apostasy"; that is, he reversed completely the purposes and principles
that had hitherto governed his writing. And as these purposes and
principles are approved, one of two conclusions follows: either that
the final scene is the product of a Marlowe in decline; or that he wrote
it, at the best, as an exercise; at the worst as a joke, with his tongue in
his cheek. There is another critic who says: "The alternative of a happy
solution lies close at hand. It is only a lingering taste for the lurid
and the horrible, ingrained in this sort of melodrama, that sends
Faustus shrieking to hell."

To both it would seem possible to reply that no scene of such
excellence—and the excellence, so far as I know, is not denied—could
issue from anyone who was not both capable of and actually exerting
his powers to the utmost. But this perhaps assumes as premiss a belief
about life and literature which, though acknowledged outside *Scrutiny*,
is not generally used as such. Therefore it is advisable to fall back on
a reply that can be verified from the words of the text; and to claim
that, so far from being disconnected from its predecessors, the final
scene refers to them continually and is continually referred to by them.

The man who is "sent shrieking to hell" is one who previously had
vaunted:

> Thinkst thou that Faustus is so fond, to imagine
> That after this life there is any paine?
> Tush, these are trifles and meere olde wives tales.

Whereas his ambition had been to

> . . . make man to live eternally,
> Or being dead, raise them to life againe,

"Faustus *as Allegory*" (*Editor's title*). *From "Marlowe's* Dr. Faustus" *by James
Smith,* Scrutiny, *VIII (1939), 36–48. Copyright 1939 by the Syndics of the Cambridge University Press. Reprinted by permission of the publisher and the author.*

he is, in the last scene, reduced to lament that he cannot die:

> Or, why is this immortall that thou hast?
> Ah *Pythagoras metemsucosis,* were that true.
> This soule should flie from me, and I be changde
> Unto some brutish beast: al beasts are happy,
> For when they die,
> Their soules are soone dissolved in elements,
> But mine must live. . . .

He finds it impossible to be rid of his soul:

> Why wert thou not a creature wanting soule?

whereas before he had thought nothing easier than to throw it away:

> Had I as many soules as there be starres,
> Ide give them all for *Mephastophilis.*

Or again:

> . . . Heres the scrowle
> Wherein thou hast given thy soule to *Lucifer.*
> —I, and body too, but what of that?

And so on: it would be possible, in illustration of this point, to transcribe whole pages of dialogue. But it is perhaps superfluous to do so, and relevant quotation will in any case be necessary later.

These references backward, once recognized, improve, I think, the last scene, however impressive in itself; and that the earlier scenes are improved by it, goes without saying. By them the play is knit into a firm if simple structure, of which it is still possible, in spite of a mutilated text, to trace the main outlines. I shall at least attempt to do so in this paper.

But first it will be necessary to discuss other and, I am afraid, more general topics. For the play makes extensive use of a system of ideas which is no longer widely familiar; and it cannot be recalled by the brief hints which, as sufficient in his time, are all that Marlowe provides.

Pared of its comic scenes, and of the not very serious ones first published in 1616, the play cannot, according to a common opinion, be interpreted wholly realistically. It is not merely a photograph, showing beings who exist side by side to influence one another. A large measure of the action takes place not so much between beings as within a single one of them, Faustus himself; of whom the Good and the Evil Angel, for example, are parts. And so, I would add, are the Old Man, Helen, Mephistophilis, even Lucifer; in a certain sense, which I shall endeavour to explain below, they are parts of Faustus. The play in other words is an allegory.

Yet obviously the Good and the Evil Angel, Helen and the rest are not merely parts of Faustus. The two angels are emissaries of powers, or representatives of orders, independent of himself; while Helen, though a shade, is more than a figment of his imagination. Hence it would appear that allegory does not altogether exclude realism; or perhaps better, that when as excellent as Marlowe's it inevitably employs realism as an instrument. For if compared with other types, its excellence will be found to be precisely this: that it is neither a puzzle, in which things are given an interest by being called other than their proper names; nor is it a scientific analysis, in which various aspects of a thing are isolated for their readier comprehension. I would say rather that it is a synthesis, rendering comprehension not so much more ready as more full.

Marlowe chooses certain characters so as to be capable of at least a double function: they are significant as symbols, in virtue of what they symbolize; but significant also as themselves, in virtue of what they are. And they are not significant now as the one thing, now as the other, by a sort of alternation; but continuously and simultaneously, as both. That they can be so, it is at least plausible to assume, is due to an affinity, or to a partial or potential identity, between what they are and what they symbolize. If the latter, establishment of the identity will be the synthesis effected. In a sense two things are distinct, and this must be acknowledged; but in a sense also they are one, and unless this is acknowledged, they cannot fully be understood, even in the sense in which they are distinct.

The Good Angel, for example, is the representative of an order or goodness, independent of Faustus in that it is not affected whether he is loyal to it or not. He can no more increase or diminish its perfection, than he can create or destroy it. But at the same time the Angel symbolizes a part of Faustus; and may do both because, though the converse is true, Faustus is by no means independent of the order. Only by loyalty can he attain his own perfection and therefore peace; if disloyal, he is tormented by regret for the perfection he has sacrificed. And so, whatever the goodness or badness of his life, the order is vindicated in him: he is evidence of it, a part of it—and to be identified with it, in this sense. But there is also a sense in which he must be kept distinct; for whereas the order's perfection is compatible with any life he may choose, only one, a good one, is compatible with his own.

All this is what the Good Angel, by multiplicity of function, is able to signify. As much Faustus as, say, reason or the power of thought, he supplies the latter, when he is loyal, with an occasion for rejoicing; if otherwise, self-reproach is as inevitable as thought. But at the same time he is none the less an angel, and as such not subject to Faustus's control: he cannot for example, as thought might, be silenced from time to time and ultimately be forgotten. So that joy and sorrow are not merely, or rather in this sense not at all, selected by Faustus for himself, according to what instinct of propriety he may possess: he suffers a sorrow which is inflicted, he receives a joy which is bestowed. Yet again, all that he receives or suffers in this way, since it comes from the Good Angel or from what the Angel represents, is in conformity with and so to speak demanded by his nature: of which the Angel continues as much as ever a part. And thus a synthesis is suggested by the allegory: that Faustus's life, though single and indivisible, is both his own and not his own. On the one hand he alone can lead it, and he cannot do other than lead it, to his profit or to his loss; on the other hand however led, it is the intimate concern of, as it is intimately concerned with, what is other than himself.

In much the same way Helen is the lust of the eyes and of the flesh, both as these are objects in an external world, other than Faustus; and as they are his own passions, leading him to seek within those objects a happiness. As both, she is able to signifiy that, by his nature, he is bound to the objects in one relation or another; inevitably they are part of his living. But the consequences of any relation are determined by the objects as distinct from his nature; and so there is a sense in which he and Helen must be distinct. While the Good Angel, at least as substantial as he, could ensure a lasting happiness; that proffered by Helen can be no more than momentary, for she is hardly substantial— she is a shade.

An allegorical interpretation of this kind should not perhaps be limited to space but extended also to time. I mean that, just as the spatial distinction between Faustus and the Good Angel is accepted as to some extent, though not wholly, a device (for while distinct, the two in another sense are one): so also should the temporal separation between his death and his signing of the contract. The one event follows the other after a period of twenty-four years, and the period is significant as itself; but also, I think, it is symbolical of the moment of signing. Or rather, of the moment at which Faustus determines to sign: for at that moment, and without delay, he plunges to spiritual death. He kills his soul, which does not need twenty-four years to weaken or to wither. But as death, whether spiritual or physical, does not annihilate a soul, the consequences of the determination to sign, though arriving within are not confined to a moment. Without the intervention of grace they will stretch through eternity, and can therefore be represented, if at all, only under some figure of time. And this is the purpose of the twenty-four years: which as has been said are significant as themselves—but are so only that a single moment may be the more adequately symbolized. To accomplish his purpose Marlowe might be said to write a play of which the hero is both alive and not alive. He appears to be working out as best he can his salvation, and in a sense he is doing so; but there is another sense in which he is working out neither his salvation nor his damnation. He is damned already.

Recognition of both these allegories, and that they are of complicated rather than simple type, is I think necessary to remove obstacles to the reader's enjoyment. For if it is not made, various absurdities arise which are incompatible with the reputation the play is felt to deserve. If for example the two Angels are accepted merely in their symbolical sense, as parts of Faustus, they are nothing but ideals or aspirations opposing one another within his brain. To one or other he must attach himself, but it is not yet obvious which; meanwhile he must behave impartially to both, since both are his offspring. And the two must argue for his allegiance; with the result that, as Mr. Santayana says, "the Good Angel . . . seems to have the worst of it." But if this is so, the last scene is not only irrelevant, it is contradictory of all that precedes; and no criticism of it could be too severe. A happy ending was demanded, to justify the sound decision of an umpire; and this Marlowe, through malice or perversity, refuses to provide.

If on the other hand the Angels are accepted as at the same time angels; as representatives, that is, of orders established in a universe outside Faustus: it cannot appear doubtful even for a moment which of them should be followed. For Faustus is submitted to the universe as its creature, though a free one; and it is precisely to express this submission that he is symbolized by the Angels at all. Of these it is assumed —or rather, it would be assumed by an Elizabethan audience—that good dominates evil, so to speak absorbs it, and subordinates the ends of evil to ends of its own. Therefore there is no hope of Faustus cutting loose from what the Good Angel represents: by refusing to co-operate with it however insistently he can only prepare for himself a future punishment—and this is a form of involuntary co-operation.

On other grounds it might be said that argument is not even possible. For Faustus, no more than another man, could be argued into a choice of evil as evil. The sole problem, given the Angels as an objective evil and an objective good, is not which of them ought to be followed; but which of them will be followed in fact, and what the consequences will be.

These are to some extent displayed by behaviour on the part of the Angels which, if at first sight it might be taken for argument, is in reality very different. It will be remembered that the consequences, though they immediately supervene, are for their fuller comprehension spread over twenty-four years. Faustus is allowed to explore evil with all patience and all diligence; so that, if it does not bring happiness,

the fact after such an experiment shall be more convincing; if on the
other hand it brings misery, the contrast with what appeared happiness
for a time shall be the sharper. During the whole of the twenty-four
years each of the Angels continues in his double role: as part of Faustus,
expressing his preoccupations; and as external agent, either encourag-
ing those preoccupations or seeking to end them. As both, the Evil
Angel and his associates—for he is not considered profitably, apart
from the devils—are inevitably more prominent in the earlier scenes.
Evil is a new toy, on which Faustus cannot cease to ponder; nor can he
resist any invitations to evil that he may receive. If it is impossible the
Good Angel should be silenced, he may at any rate be reduced to single
lines and general warnings, such as are easily ignored.

> Sweet Faustus, thinke of heaven and heavenly things.
> —No Faustus, thinke of honor and of wealth.
> —Of wealth,
> Why the signiory of Embden shall be mine.

This is not an argument, by which Faustus or anyone is to be per-
suaded that evil is better than good; but a mere statement or illustration
of the fact that, once Faustus has chosen evil, he has neither eyes nor
ears save for the immediate advantages of having done so.

The gifts of the devil however neither satisfy nor last. Power and
wealth, all that Faustus hitherto has obtained, are not in themselves
either bad or good; and so long as they are contemplated merely, he
need not be disturbed. But once the attempt is made to use them, disillusion begins. In his inexperience he thinks that, having sold himself
into hell, he will be allowed to retain a portion of his integrity: to
seize the opportunity, for example, of new found wealth, to set up an
orderly household. Therefore he asks for a wife, and one is brought.
But she proves stuffed with fireworks and goes up in smoke:

> A plague on her for a hote whore,

he cries, and must henceforth content himself with the "fairest curte-
zans."

Thus his fleshly desires are satisfied, *tant bien que mal;* but the result
is that his spiritual desires, as they are the more isolated, become the
more insistent. The devil, having already supplied a book of spells, of
planets and of herbs, is summoned to dispute of "divine astrologie."
The joy of learning, however, is no more permissible to Faustus than
that of domestic bliss; for if pursued in due order and in the proper
temper, it can lead to one thing only—the knowledge, the love and
ultimately the vision of God. And all these, along with goodness, he
has renounced. By a process of reasoning which resembles, and is

probably intended to recall, the scholastic argument *a contingentia,*
Faustus ascends from a consideration of the planets to that of the moving Intelligences; and thence to the supreme Intelligence which is the
origin and mover of all.

> Tell me who made the world?

he asks, but can receive no answer. The whole economy of hell is disturbed; Lucifer appears with his "companion prince," Beelzebub, and
"looking terrible" imposes silence. But as Faustus's mind cannot be
left completely vacant there is offered him, as a substitute for the vision
of God, that of the seven deadly sins. He watches with detachment, but
not without interest; for if he is moved to no protest against their
loathsomeness, he exchanges quips with one or two. And at the end he
exclaims:

> O this feedes my soule.
> —Tut Faustus, in hel is al manner of delight.
> —O might I see hel, and return againe, how happy were I then?

At this point he has fallen victim to a vice familiar to the Fathers
and to the schoolmen, but rarely mentioned as such today: that of
curiosity. "Whereas the voluptuous man," says Augustine, "seeks after
what is beautiful, melodious, sweet or smooth, the curious man seeks
after the very opposites of these; not however that he may be vexed by
them, but merely out of the lust to experience and to know." This is
Faustus's case: the seven sins do not move him as they would an ordinary man, and as a man should be moved. He has begun to collect
sensations without judgment and without order, not as an aid to right
living but merely for their own sake. And the further descent from
curiosity of the senses to that of the intellect is easy. "No longer"—to
quote Augustine once again—"is nature explored only so far as is necessary to see the eternal through the temporal," but ransacked in all its
corners for the quicker compassing of "false and earthly happiness,
empty and worldly distinction." With the magazines of science which
Faustus now accumulates, he is out of the danger of knowing God; he
is on the other hand the better qualified to tease Popes, oblige Duches-
ses and entertain Emperors.

In the passage from which the last quotation comes, and also elsewhere, Augustine connects curiosity with the conjuring and worship of
devils. It is not only this which leads to the suspicion that he, or at least
his doctrines, had a strong influence on *Dr. Faustus* (a direct influence
I mean, and not only by way of the *Faustbook;* for as will be apparent
now or later, I think Marlowe abandons the theology of the *Faustbook*
for one which is more humane, as it is more traditional). That the un-

bounded appetite for experience or for learning was a discovery of the
Renaissance is a superstition common amongst commentators: it had
however been known long before, and in particular to Augustine—who
was seduced into Manichaeism by the promise he would no longer need
to believe, but should know; and who had, in his own magnificent
image, the "sun and moon served up to him in a dish," but found the
food unsustaining. What was new in the Renaissance was the neglect of
the boundaries within which, as had been taught by considered experience, this appetite must be guided if it were not to lead to disaster.
And thus if any step was taken by Marlowe's contemporaries it was
backward (in this matter at least) rather than forward. Marlowe also
may have taken the step in *Tamburlaine,* and it seems probable that
he did; but if so, he was seeking in *Dr. Faustus* to recover lost ground
as speedily as possible. For evidence in support of this it is necessary
to consider only the verse of the two plays, especially of the death
scenes. They cannot be held—or rather they should not be held, for
it seems they often are—to be mere repetitions one of another *in
dispari materia*: the latter is immeasurably more mature. It is indeed
fully mature, while the other, like the Renaissance in so many aspects,
is no more than adolescent.

But this is a digression. The eternal, which we left Faustus neglect-
ing, in the end cannot but avenge itself; for its only rival must sooner
or later vanish, leaving an open field. By the choice of evil Faustus
has forfeited not only spiritual but physical integrity, such as in the
allegory is destroyed by the passage of time. An Old Man ("base and
crooked age," that is *Senectus*) reminds him of this. Unable to deny
it he is as never before seized with fury against an agent of good, and
asks for him to be tormented. But in vain: for Mephistophilis is power-
less against one who, unlike Faustus, has laid fast hold on the eternal:

> My faith, vile hel, shall triumph over thee.
> Ambitious fiends, see how the heavens smiles
> At your repulse, and laughs your state to scorn.
> Hence hel, for hence I flie unto my God.

Faustus on the contrary has nowhere to fly but to what remains of
his youth; the more fleeting as youth itself is a shadow. Helen plays
Juventus, and it is of her that he is driven to beg

> Sweet *Helen,* make me immortal with a kiss;

meaning thereby not that he himself—for to his misfortune, he is
immortal already—but that what remains of youth, the present moment, shall not pass away. By the nature of things this is impossible;
the twenty-four years draw to a close and before the allegory ends
the last gift of the Evil Angel—for which in turn all others have been

sacrificed, and all that might have come from any other source—has already crumbled in his hands.

As the attractiveness of evil gradually declines, that of good grows in inverse proportion. For it is eternal and therefore remains to draw Faustus's eyes when, the mists of evil dissolved, they are left hungry for an object. Thus the more prominent role which in the earlier scenes fell to the Evil Angel, is in the later assumed by the Good Angel and his associates: the Old Man and Faustus's own conscience. The latter, who once confined the Good Angel to the briefest of utterances, in the penultimate scene is himself forced to exclaim at length:

> What wonders I have done al *Germany* can witness, yea all the world, for which *Faustus* hath lost both *Germany,* and the world, yea heaven it selfe, heaven the seate of God the throne of the blessed, the king- dome of joy, and must remain in hel for ever, hel, ah, hel for ever, sweete friends, what shall become of Faustus, being in hel for ever? . . . Ah Gentlemen! I gave my soule for my cunning.—God forbid.—God forbade it indeed, but Faustus hath done it: for vaine pleasure of 24. yeares hath Faustus lost eternall joy and felicitie.

The Good Angel "gets the best of it" after all; for he or his allies speak last and, as this is not an argument but a history, he who speaks last wins.

Having forfeited the good, Faustus's knowledge of it is of course in no sense full; still, there is a degree of which he cannot be rid, sufficient to feed a regret which is his chief torment in eternity. According to Mephistophilis it is also the torment of the devils, who nevertheless do not lack diligence in or affection to evil. The two therefore—the regret and the affection—are not incompatible; and this notion may perhaps be of use in removing what appears another misunderstanding of Mr. Santayana's.

"The excellent Faustus," he complains, ". . . is browbeaten by the devil and forbidden to repent when he has actually repented." But if so the play, as containing a contradiction, could hardly be taken seriously; or at least, no more seriously than is its source the *Faust- book,* to which Mr. Santayana's words more certainly apply. Even admirers of the latter would perhaps admit this to be a mistake; and there is I think in the play, over and above what there is in the book, something which Mr. Santayana overlooks—once again, the allegories. In so far as Marlowe's Faustus is damned, and as he is living on earth only to exemplify in part the sufferings of the damned, he has identi- fied himself with the devils as far as he possibly can. And he is kept to hell, or to association with evil, exactly as they are: not by brow- beatings and prohibitions, but by his own free will. For they have an affection to evil; they have so formed or deformed themselves that they can desire only what secures them misery. Had they for example the opportunity to escape from hell they would not take it; though it is a place only of suffering, such as comes from the loss of heaven. Rather than not have heaven in hell where alone it is impossible, they would not have it at all. A state of violent discord and disorder similar to this exists in Faustus's soul. And this is what passages like the following, which Mr. Santayana has in mind, are intended to convey allegorically. It is not only Lucifer who drags a reluctant Faustus from thoughts of heaven:

> Ah Christ my Saviour,
> Seeke to save distressed Faustus soule.
> —Christ cannot save thy soule, for he is just,
> Thers none but I have intrest in the same.
> —O who art thou that lookst so terrible?
> —I am Lucifer. . . .
> We come to tell thee thou dost injure us.
> Thou talkst of Christ, contrary to thy promise:
> Thou shouldst not thinke of God, thinke of the devil,
> And of his dame too.

Faustus also drags himself. For Lucifer, like the Good Angel, is here playing a double role: he is devil, but also he is part of Faustus, who is thus agent as well as victim in his own torment. And an interpretation of this kind should always I think be made whenever, at first sight, it appears that Faustus's moral freedom is being infringed. It is not, for example, only Lucifer and Beelzebub who forbid him to continue the study of "astrologie"; it is his own evil will, which has already determined not to embrace the truths to which astrology is leading. To do this he has to exert violence on himself, not inaptly represented by a disturbance in hell; principally he has to sink deeper into hell, or to reveal a greater depth of evil in himself than has yet appeared. And as has been seen, this is what he does.

It is of course impossible to get a clear conception of his state; eternity is full of contradictions, so is evil, and little perspicuity is to be expected of a notion that combines the two. But Marlowe comes perhaps as near to a forcible expression of it as possible. Because of its complication his allegory is so to speak more than an allegory: one picture is not substituted for and therefore weakened by another; two pictures are retained, to give each other strength. Faustus suffers not merely *as though* he were struggling with an outside enemy, he has such an enemy; not merely *as though* he were torn within, he is so torn. And against Lucifer he must struggle with the persistence called for against himself: against himself with the violence for which

Lucifer calls. The whole of his strength seems to lie on both sides
of the struggle and therefore he is indeed, as he says, torn as by devils.
But he should also add that he had an affection to the devils which
tears equally.

The temporal allegory is effective in a very similar way. We can
conceive of pain or sorrow persisting at its acutest only in the hope
that one day it will cease: otherwise it must either blunt itself, or wear
out its possessor. As he is alive Faustus has hope, and therefore pain
of this intensity:

> Ah Christ my Saviour,
> Seeke to save distressed Faustus soule.

But at the same time he has no hope, for he is dead:

> I am Lucifer. . . .
> Thou talkst of Christ contrary to thy promise,
> . . . thinke of the devil.

This does not of course mean that he unites contradictories in himself, as life and death; but that, since his life illustrates his death,
he must be conceived as continuing after death to suffer the utmost
that, in life, he has ever suffered. Yet the one condition, that of hope,
has disappeared, which as far as our experience goes makes such suffering supportable.

It should perhaps be further noted that the allegories not only provide material and machinery for the body of the play, but shape it.
It begins with a monologue, for example, and ends with one: as
Faustus alone can commit the act for which he is to be punished, he
enters alone to commit it so that responsibility shall be clear. He
alone can endure the punishment, and is therefore left alone to meet
it. But between these two points the stage is crowded with figures who,
if they cannot commit may influence the act; or if not influence, may
be influenced by it: the more fully to exhibit its nature and its workings. Only towards the end the stage thins out, and Faustus is left
alone with his Scholars. They are little more than conveniences, to allow him to soliloquize in public: the solitude which he dreads nevertheless pursuing him, and so to speak commanding him to itself out
of society. Similarly with the allegory of time. In the body of the
play scene succeeds scene, not indeed in any order, but in one which
is more of psychological than chronological significance. They are like
tableaux, illustrating the possibly simultaneous aspects of a man's
state of soul, rather than events in his history. But towards the end
references to time begin to multiply: Faustus must back to Wittenberg, he must nurse his complacency with a "quiet sleep," soon sleep
will not suffice and he is driven to riot and debauch. In the final

monologue a clock is on the stage, faster than ordinary clocks; its
second half-hour is shorter than its first; and Faustus's imagery, now
seeking to halt time, now yielding to it in despair, only succeeds in
making it fly the faster:

> The starres moove stil, time runs, the clocke wil strike,
> The divel wil come, and Faustus must be damnd.

The Damnation of Faustus

by Helen Gardner

We are all familiar with the progeny of Milton's Satan and the effort of most recent criticism has been directed towards clearing the Satan of Milton's poem from his associations with the Promethean rebel of romantic tradition. But the question whether Satan had any ancestors has hardly been raised, or has been dismissed by reference to the devil of popular tradition, or by an allusion to the heroic figure of the Old English *Genesis B*. The late Mr. Charles Williams, in an essay on Milton which seems likely to become a classic, and Mr. C. S. Lewis, building, as he delighted to own, on Mr. Williams, destroyed, one hopes for ever, the notion that Satan had grounds for his rebellion.[1] But when we have agreed that Satan's "wrongs" which "exceed all measure" exist only in Shelley's generous imagination, and that it is easier to draw a bad character than a good, and have assented to the statement that Satan's career is a steady progress from bad to worse and ends with his complete deformity, we still have no explanation of why the Romantic critics stood *Paradise Lost* on its head, or why the "common reader" finds the imaginative impact of the first books so much more powerful than that of the last, or why, as one re-reads the poem, the exposure of Satan's malice and meanness seems curiously irrelevant. There remains always, untouched by the argument, the image of enormous pain and eternal loss. It is out of key with the close of the poem, which does not drive it from our memory, nor absorb it.

"From hero to general, from general to politician, from politician to secret service agent, and thence to a thing that peers in at bedroom

"The Damnation of Faustus" (*Editor's title*). *From "Milton's Satan and the Theme of Damnation in Elizabethan Tragedy" by Helen Gardner,* English Studies 1948 (*Vol. I, 1948, of the new series of* Essays and Studies), *pp. 46–53, with revision as provided by the author in her appendix to* A Reading of Paradise Lost (*Oxford: Clarendon Press, 1965; New York: Oxford University Press, 1965*), *pp. 99–120. Reprinted by permission of the author and Oxford University Press.*

[1] See *The English Poems of Milton,* with a preface by Charles Williams, (World's Classics) 1940, and C. S. Lewis, *A Preface to Paradise Lost,* 1942.

or bathroom windows, and thence to a toad, and finally to a snake—
such is the progress of Satan," writes Mr. Lewis, and he rightly declares
that there is no question of Milton's beginning by making Satan too
glorious and then, too late, attempting to rectify the error. "Such an
unerring picture of 'the sense of injured merit' in its actual operations
upon character cannot have come about by blundering and accident."
We can parallel this account of the career of Satan, but not from Iago
and Becky Sharp, whom Mr. Lewis cites as examples of bad characters
who are more interesting than their virtuous opposites. From a brave
and loyal general, to a trecherous murderer, to a hirer of assassins, to
an employer of spies, to a butcher, to a coward, to a thing with no
feeling for anything but itself, to a monster and a "hell-hound": that
is a summary of the career of Macbeth. From a proud philosopher,
master of all human knowledge, to a trickster, to a slave of phantoms,
to a cowering wretch: that is a brief sketch of the progress of Dr.
Faustus. With varying use of mythological machinery, this theme of
the deforming of a creature in its origin bright and good, by its own
willed persistence in acts against its own nature, is handled by Shakespeare and Marlowe, and with great power, but in a purely naturalistic setting, by Middleton and Rowley in *The Changeling*. It is on the
tragic stage that we find the idea of damnation in English literature
before *Paradise Lost*. "Satan," writes Mr. Williams, "is the Image of
personal clamour for personal independence." He is in rebellion
against "the essential fact of things." The same can be said of Faustus,
of Macbeth, and of Beatrice-Joanna, and it is particularly interesting
to notice that in *Macbeth* and *The Changeling* the dramatists have
altered their sources to bring out the full implications of the theme.

The devil was a comic character in the medieval drama; in the
Elizabethan period he virtually disappears in his own person from the
greater plays. But what Mr. Lewis calls "the Satanic predicament" is
there, and it appears in the tragic, not the comic mode of vision. The
terrible distinction between devils and men in popular theology lay
in the irreversibility of the fall of the angels. Unlike men the fallen
angels were incapable of repentance and so for them there was no
pardon. As Donne puts it: "To those that fell, can appertaine no
reconciliation; no more then to those that die in their sins; for *Quod
homini mors, Angelis casus;* The fall of the Angels wrought upon
them, as the death of a man does upon him; They are both equally
incapable of change to better." [2] Donne recognizes that some of the
Fathers thought that "the devill retaining still his faculty of free will,
is therefore capable of repentance, and so of benefit by this comming

---

[2] *LXXX Sermons*, 1640, p. 9. A recent reading of Donne's *Sermons* for another
purpose has impressed upon me how often Donne provides the comment of a
theologian or a moralist upon the tragedies of his contemporaries.

of Christ";[3] but this is exactly the point which Aquinas denies and Donne assents to his view. Aquinas decides that the fallen angels cannot repent, since, though they know the beginnings of penitence in fear, their free-will is perverted: "Quid-quid in eis est naturale, totum est bonum et ad bonum inclinans, sed liberum arbitrium in eis est in malo obstinatum; et quia motus virtutis et vitii non sequitur inclinationem naturae, sed magis motum liberi arbitrii; ideo non oportet, quamvis naturaliter inclinentur ad bonum, quod motus virtutis in eis sit, vel esse possit." [4] In the tragic world of Faustus and Macbeth we find presented to us in human terms this incapacity for change to a better state. It never occurs to us that Macbeth will turn back, or indeed that he can; and though Marlowe, in this more merciful, as he is always more metaphysical, than Shakespeare, keeps before us the fact of Faustus's humanity by the urgings of the Good Angel, yet to the Good Angel's "Faustus, repent; yet God will pity thee," comes at once the Bad Angel's response: "Thou art a spirit;[5] God cannot pity thee"; and to Faustus's

> Who buzzeth in mine ears, I am a spirit?
> Be I a devil, yet God may pity me;
> Yea, God will pity me, if I repent.

comes the confident statement of the Bad Angel: "Ay, but Faustus never shall repent"; to which Faustus gives a despairing assent: "My heart is harden'd, I cannot repent." [6]

In the three plays mentioned, along with this incapacity for change to a better state, or repentance, go two other closely related ideas. The initial act is an act against nature, it is a primal sin, in that it contradicts the "essential fact of things," and its author knows that it does so. It is not an act committed by mistake; it is not an error of judgment, it is an error of will. The act is unnatural and so are its results; it deforms the nature which performs it. The second idea is the irony

---

[3] *Ibid.*, p. 66.
[4] *S.T.*, Supplement, Q. XVI, Art. 3.
[5] *Spirit* here as elsewhere in the play means evil spirit, or devil.
[6] All quotations from *Dr. Faustus* are from the edition of Dr. F. S. Boas, 1932. The point that Faustus is presented to us as incapable of real repentance, though like the devils he knows the beginnings of penitence in fear and "believes and trembles," is obscured if we accept, as Dr. Boas does, the suggestion of Mr. H. T. Baker (*Modern Language Notes*, vol. XXI, pp. 86–7) and transfer to Faustus the close of the Old Man's Speech in Act v, scene i (p. 161). In this most touching scene the Old Man makes a last appeal to Faustus to remember his humanity:

> Though thou hast now offended like a man,
> Do not persever in it like a devil;
> Yet, yet, thou hast an amiable soul,
> If sin by custom grow not into nature.

of retributive justice. The act is performed for an imagined good, which appears so infinitely desirable that the conditions for its supposed satisfaction are accepted; but a rigorous necessity reigns and sees to it that though the conditions are exacted literally, the desire is only granted ironically, and this is inevitable, since the desire is for something forbidden by the very nature of man.[7]

We are unfortunate in possessing Marlowe's greatest play only in an obviously mutilated form; but in spite of possible distortion and some interpolation in the centre, the grandeur of the complete reversal stands out clearly. Apart from its opening and concluding choruses, which provide an archaic framework, and the short closing scene in the 1616 text, where the scholars find the mangled body of Faustus, the play begins and ends with the hero in his study. In the first scene Faustus runs through all the branches of human knowledge and finds them inadequate to his desires. Logic can only teach argument; medicine stops short where human desire is most thwarted, since it cannot defeat death; law is a mercenary pursuit, and divinity, which he comes to last, holds the greatest disappointment: it is grounded in the recognition of man's mortality and his fallibility. The two texts from Jerome's Bible insult his aspiration: *Stipendium peccati mors est,* and *Si peccasse negamus, fallimur, et nulla est in nobis veritas.*[8] He turns instead to magic because it is

> a world of profit and delight,
> Of power, of honour, and omnipotence.

He decides to "tire his brains to get a deity." The sin of Faustus here is presumption, the aspiring above his order, or the rebellion against the law of his creation.

But when he is last seen alone in his study it is the opposite sin which delivers him to damnation: the final sin of Faustus is despair.[9]

---

[7] Donne supplies us with a comment on the "omnipotence" of Faustus, the "kingship" of Macbeth and the "marriage" of Beatrice-Joanna, when he says: "For small wages, and ill-paid pensions we serve him (Satan); and lest any man should flatter and delude himselfe, in saying, I have my wages, and my reward before hand, my pleasures in this life, the punishment, (if ever) not till the next, The Apostle destroyes that dreame, with that question of confusion, *What fruit had you then in those things, of which you are now ashamed?* Certainly sin is not a gainfull way; . . . fruitlesness, unprofitableness before, shame and dishonor after." *LXXX Sermons,* p. 65.

[8] It is worth noting that Faustus does not complete the text, which is familiar from its use as one of the Sentences. "If we say that we have no sin, we deceive ourselves, and the truth is not in us: but, if we confess our sins, he is faithful and just to forgive us our sins, and to cleanse us from all unrighteousness."

[9] The word *despair* or its derivative *desperate* occurs thirteen times in the play. See i. 3. 91; ii. 1. 4 and 5; ii. 2. 25 and 31; iv. 5a, 31; v. 1. 64, 68, 72 and 79; v. 2. 11, 92 and 101.

In *The Conflict of Conscience* by Nathaniell Woodes, Minister of Norwich, pub-

However much he may call in his fear on God or Christ, it is the power
of Lucifer and the bond with Lucifer which he really believes in. It
is to Lucifer he prays: "O, spare me, Lucifer!", and "Ah, rend not my
heart for naming of my Christ!" Donne gives presumption and despair
as one of the couples which the Schoolmen have called sins against
the Holy Ghost "because naturally they shut out those meanes by
which the Holy Ghost might work upon us . . . for presumption
takes away the feare of God, and desperation the love of God." [10] They
are the two faces of the sin of Pride. Faustus tormented by devils is
obsessed by their power; but the Old Man is safe from them, because
of his faith. The great reversal from the first scene of *Dr. Faustus* to
the last can be defined in different ways: from presumption to despair;
from doubt of the existence of hell to belief in the reality of nothing
else; from a desire to be more than man to the recognition that he
has excluded himself from the promise of redemption for all mankind
in Christ; from haste to sign the bond to desire for delay when the
moment comes to honour it; from aspiration to deity and omnipotence
to longing for extinction. At the beginning Faustus wished to rise
above his humanity; at the close he would sink below it, be transformed into a beast or into "little water drops." At the beginning he
attempts usurpation upon God; at the close he is an usurper upon the
Devil.[11]

---

lished 1581 (Hazlitt-Dodsley, vol. VI) in which we can see the old morality play
of wrongful choice, punishment, repentance and forgiveness turning into the
Elizabethan tragedy of sin and retribution, the whole struggle in the final act is
between the hero's despair and the efforts of his friends to convince him that he
is not beyond God's mercy. One can commend the enterprise if not the success
of the Minister of Norwich in trying to put the finer points of the doctrine of
justification by faith into fourteeners. Poor as his play is, it shows in a most
interesting way the great debate of the sixteenth and seventeenth centuries on the
freedom of the will being turned into drama. In *The Conflict of Conscience*, at
the very last moment, faith conquers, and the happy ending of the old morality is
preserved. [When I wrote this I was unaware that the play is found in two issues.
As originally published it ended, as in life, with the hero (Francis Spira) commit-
ing suicide. In the second issue his name was removed from the title-page and a
happy ending was substituted. See the Malone Society reprint.] In *Dr. Faustus*,
which retains formally much of the old morality, despair triumphs. Our understanding of some of the tragedies of Shakespeare and his contemporaries might be
enriched if we thought more in terms of

Providence, Foreknowledge, Will, and Fate,
Fixt Fate, free will, foreknowledge absolute,

and less in terms of "fatal flaws" and "errors of judgment."

[10] *LXXX Sermons*, p. 349.

[11] "The greatest sin that ever was, and that upon which even the blood of
Christ Jesus hath not wrought, the sin of Angels was that, *Similis ero Altissimo*,
to be like God. To love our selves, to be satisfied in our selves, to finde an omnisuf-
ficiency in our selves, is an intrusion, an usurpation upon God." *Ibid.*, p. 156. "Did

As for the reward Faustus obtains, it is difficult to argue from the play as it has come down to us, and one should not in fairness say that Faustus appears to sell his soul for the satisfaction of playing practical jokes. But there are two episodes of some significance near the beginning, in which Marlowe's hand is clearly apparent, which it is possible to argue from. Faustus takes Mephistophilis as his servant; he demands twenty-four years of "all voluptuousness"

> Having thee ever to attend on me,
> To give me whatsoever I shall ask,
> To tell me whatsoever I demand,
>
> .   .   .   .
>
> And always be obedient to my will.

As the play proceeds it is clear what happens with the last clause of the agreement: the obedient servant becomes the master. It is Mephistophilis who speaks with authority as representative of "great Lucifer" and it is Faustus who obeys. But it is the same with the other two clauses. Immediately after the bond is signed Faustus begins to ask questions, and he asks about hell. He receives what are in the context of the play true answers, but he does not believe them. He thinks hell a fable, and Mephistophilis with melancholy irony leaves the subject: "Ay, think so, till experience change thy mind." Then Faustus makes his first request: he asks for a wife. Here the text is plainly defective; the verse breaks down into half-lines and prose, a devil enters dressed as a woman with fireworks attached which explode. But after this horseplay, Mephistophilis resumes in dignified Marlovian verse:

> Marriage is but a ceremonial toy:
> And if thou lovest me, think no more of it.
> I'll cull thee out the fairest courtesans,
> And bring them ev'ry morning to thy bed:
> She whom thine eye shall like, thy heart shall have.

If we turn to the source, the English Faust Book, we can, I think, see the implications of the scene and conjecture why Marlowe set it here.

God ordain hell fire for us? no, but for the Devil and his Angels. And yet we that are vessels so broken, as that there is not a sheard left, to fetch water at the pit, that is, no means in our selves, to derive one drop of Christs blood upon us, nor to wring out one tear of true repentance from us, have plung'd our selves into this everlasting, and this dark fire, which was not prepared for us: A wretched covetousness, to be intruders upon the Devil; a wretched ambition, to be usurpers upon damnation." *XXVI Sermons,* 1660, p. 273.

Doctor *Faustus* . . . bethinking himselfe of a wife called *Mephi-stophiles* to counsaile; which would in no wise agree: demanding of him if he would breake the couenant made with him or if hee had forgot it. Hast thou not (quoth *Mephistophiles*) sworne thy selfe an enemy to God and all creatures? To this I answere thee, thou canst not marry; thou canst not serue two masters, God, and my Prince: for wedlock is a chiefe institution ordained of God, and that hast thou promised to defie, as we doe all, and that hast thou also done: and moreouer thou hast confirmed it with thy blood: perswade thy selfe, that what thou doost in contempt of wedlock, it is all to thine owne delight.

When Faustus persists in his demand, an ugly devil appears and offers himself as a bride. On his vanishing Mephistophilis re-appears to say: "It is no iesting with us, holde thou that which thou hast vowed, and wee will perform as wee haue promised." [12] The point of the scene is clear even in the play as we have it: Faustus' first request is met with a refusal. The source gives the full implications of that refusal, which may have been cut out to allow for more fireworks: marriage and "the fairest courtesans" are incompatibles. Faustus has not exchanged limitations for freedom; he has merely exchanged one kind of limitation for another. Marriage belongs to the world he has left. He cannot have all he wants, for the satisfaction of some desires involves the thwarting of others.

It is the same with knowledge soon after. Faustus disputes with Mephistophilis of "divine astrology." The answers he gets he dismisses with contempt; he knew them already. But then he goes on to ask the great question:

> *Faust.* Well, I am answer'd. Now tell me who made the world.
> *Meph.* I will not.
> *Faust.* Sweet Mephistophilis, tell me.
> *Meph.* Move me not, Faustus.
> *Faust.* Villain, have I not bound thee to tell me any thing?
> *Meph.* Ay, that is not against our kingdom.
> This is: thou art damn'd; think thou of hell.

Some kinds of knowledge, like some kinds of experience, Faustus has shut himself off from. He has not escaped the necessity of choice. It is a chosen path he follows to the end. Marlowe does all he can by the device of the two angels to keep before us that Faustus is still a man, and that repentance is open to him, if he will only

> Call for mercy, and avoid despair.

[12] *Dr. Faustus*, ed. cit, Appendix I, pp. 181–2.

But he persists. His rewards are the delights of the imagination, sweet and terrible fantasies, culminating in the vision of Helen,[13] and the exercise of what power Mephistophilis allows him, for the practical jokes probably represent a debasing rather than an alteration of Marlowe's intention. But knowledge and felicity he has exchanged for shadows, and for power he gets slavery.

[13] Dr. Greg has recently recovered for us the full mingling of horror and beauty in the scene in which Faustus embracing Helen cries: "Her lips suck forth my soul: see where it flies!" He points out that Helen is a "spirit" and that in this play a spirit is a devil. "Faustus commits the sin of demoniality, that is bodily intercourse with demons." See W. W. Greg, "The Damnation of Faustus," *Modern Language Review* (April 1946), pp. 97–107.

The Design of *Doctor Faustus*

by Harry Levin

Large allowances should be made for the mangled and encrusted form in which *Doctor Faustus* has survived. Its very popularity seems to have subjected it to an inordinate amount of cutting and gagging and all the other indignities that dramatic texts are heir to. It was not published until 1604, more than a decade after Marlowe's death; this first quarto and later editions based on it seem to represent an unauthorized abridgment. The quarto of 1616 and others deriving from it seem to stem independently from a fuller and more authoritative manuscript, upon which editors are inclined to place increasing weight. Unfortunately, neither one—nor the combination of both— is satisfactory. The 1616 text contains about half again as much material, and preserves the play in clearer and firmer structure; yet much of that construction is filled in by an inferior hand, and several important passages are omitted. These we know from the 1604 text, which is the one most frequently reprinted; and since it is so terse a condensation, it can be very handily performed; yet it is not devoid of extraneous matter, while some of its scenes are misplaced or unduly telescoped. The recent parallel edition of Sir Walter Greg does justice, at least, to the complexity of the problem. Moreover Sir Walter confirms, with his considerable authority, the tendency to push the dating ahead to the latest period in Marlowe's career. The argument for 1592, after the publication of the *Faustbook,* seems cogent—though it carries the surprising consequence of making *Doctor Faustus* the follower rather than the forerunner of Greene's *Friar Bacon and Friar Bungay.* Even more perplexing is the enigma of Marlowe's collaboration. Not that there seems to be much disagreement about the identity of his collaborator, Samuel Rowley. But why should Rowley's clumsy journeywork eke out the greatest masterwork the English theater had thus far seen? It seems unlikely, from what Kyd tells us, that Marlowe could have worked in harness with Rowley. Was his *Doctor Faustus,*

"*The Design of* Doctor Faustus" (*Editor's title*). *From* The Overreacher: A Study of Christopher Marlowe *by Harry Levin (Cambridge, Massachusetts: Harvard University Press, 1952), pp. 121–32. Copyright © 1952 by the President and Fellows of Harvard College. Reprinted by permission of the publisher.*

then, a fragment like *Hero and Leander*? If so, was it left unfinished
at his death, or had he dropped it somewhere along the wayside? All
too understandably, he might have found his task an uncomfortable
one. Was he inhibited from finishing it by some psychological complication, or by some more instrumental reason equally inscrutable at
this date?

In spite of its uneven texture, we must view the play as a whole,
since its total design is not less meaningful than its purple passages,
and textual disintegration will not improve its fragmentary condition.
Critics have questioned the authenticity of the comic scenes, on the
grounds that Marlowe lacked a sense of humor—a premise which they
support by begging the question, and denying his authorship whenever they are confronted with a humorous speech. Marlowe's laughter,
to be sure, is not Shakespeare's; yet, as *The Jew of Malta* must have
shown us, his wit has a salt of its own. Furthermore, Elizabethan
tragedy delegates a conventional function to comedy, and *Doctor
Faustus* need be no exception to that rule. Thus Wagner, the clever
servant, mimics his master in chopping logic with the other students.
He remarks, immediately after the scene in which Faustus has bargained with Mephostophilis, that the Clown "would giue his soule to
the Diuel for a shoulder of mutton" (359). Similarly, the hostlers,
Rafe and Robin, burlesque the conjuration of Dr. Faustus; their
scene, which is out of place in the 1604 text, should come after the
scene in which Mephostophilis provides Faustus with conjuring books;
for Robin, it appears, has just stolen one of those potent volumes;
and Rafe, with its help, expects to seduce Nan Spit the kitchenmaid,
even as Faustus' necromancy will capture the love of Helen of Troy.
Before this comedy team joined Marlowe's dramatis personæ, Rafe
and Robin had parts in Lyly's *Galatea,* where they played their pranks
with alchemist's equipment; but there they had little connection with
the main plot, while their roles are intrinsic—if not essential—to
Doctor Faustus. And while the comic underplot reduces the main plot
of Marlowe's drama to absurdity, the overplot is luminously adum-
brated—sketched, as it were, in lightning against a black sky. It is the
adumbration of Faustus' downfall, glimpsed in the aboriginal tragedy
of the fallen archangel. Victor Hugo's formulation for western art, the
intermixture of grotesque and sublime, could not adduce a more
pertinent example.

How grandly all is planned! (*Wie gross ist alles angelegt!*) Goethe's
appreciation of *Doctor Faustus,* as recorded by Crabb Robinson, must
refer primarily to its conception. In its execution, it adheres somewhat too faithfully to the undramatic sequence of the *Faustbook.* The
opening scenes are necessarily explicit in underlining the conditions of
the pact; but, as a result, the play is half over before the document is

ratified and Faustus can start out upon his adventures. Out of the 1,485 lines in the 1604 Quarto, 791 have gone by before he leaves Wittenberg for Rome. The 1616 Quarto augments the ensuing scenes and links them loosely together with allusions to the papal-imperial struggle, which Rowley apparently gathered from Foxe's *Book of Martyrs*. But both versions move anticlimactically from the Pope and the Emperor to the Duchess of Vanholt and the trivial incident of the grapes. This, in the text of 1604, concludes a scene which commences at the Emperor's court and includes midway the buffooneries of the Horse-Courser. Faustus is well advised to pause for an instant and meditate on the restless course of time. Such drastic telescoping seems to indicate an acting version constrained by the narrow resources of a touring company. It is divided into fourteen continuous scenes, whereas the text of 1616 is subdivided into twenty scenes which editors distribute among five acts. Viewed in outline, the plot is perfectly classical in its climactic ascent: the conjuration of Mephostophilis, the compact with Lucifer, the travels to Rome and elsewhere, the necromantic evocations, and the casatrophe. Faustus' rise is harder to triangulate than the careers of Marlowe's other heroes, because each worldly step is a spiritual lapse. Examined more technically, the play has a strong beginning and an even stronger end; but its middle section, whether we abridge it or bombast it out with Rowley's hack-work, is unquestionably weak. The structural weakness, however, corresponds to the anticlimax of the parable; it lays bare the gap between promise and fruition, between the bright hopes of the initial scene and the abysmal consequences of the last. "As the outline of the character is grand and daring," William Hazlitt has said, "the execution is abrupt and fearful."

At the request of the emperor, Faustus has evoked no less a shade than Alexander the Great, archetype of *libido dominandi*. For the edification and pleasure of the scholars, when he returns to the university, he evokes the archetype of *libido sentiendi*. Among all the beautiful women who ever lived, they have agreed that Helen of Troy is peerless, "the pride of natures workes," the "onely Paragon of excellence" (1268). Disputation is silenced when she makes her fugitive appearance in their incongruous quarters. Since the days when Marlowe studied the classics at Cambridge, Helen had been his cynosure of comparison—comparison with Zenocrate in *Tamburlaine* and even with Gaveston in *Edward II*. But metaphor is never enough for Marlowe; he must have the real thing, beauty in person; in *The Jew of Malta* policy was personified by Machiavelli himself; and the consummation of Faustus' desire—or the consolation, at any rate, for his regret—is to have Helen as his paramour. Mephostophilis produces her "in twinckling of an eie" (1327); and the glamor of the subsequent lines has obscured this interesting verbal coinage of Marlowe's, an apt phrase for a magician's assistant engaged in bringing off his employer's most spectacular trick. This, of all occasions, is the one to which language must rise; and, in so doing, it brilliantly redeems the shortcomings of previous episodes. The apostrophe to Helen stands out from its context, not because anthologists excerpt it, but because Marlowe carefully designed it to be a set piece, a purple passage, a supreme invitation to love. Its lyrical formality, its practiced handling of stylistic and prosodic devices from his established repertory, set it off from the pithy prose, the sharp dialectic, the nervous colloquies and rhythmic variations of his maturing style. Characteristically, it does not offer any physical description of the heroine. It estimates, as Homer did, her impact. How should Faustus react to the sight that had stirred the elders of Troy to forget their arguments in admiration? Chapman would render their winged words in his *Iliad*:

> What man can blame
> The Greekes and Trojans to endure, for so Admir'd a Dame,
> So many miseries, and so long? In her sweet countenance shine
> Lookes like the Goddesses.   (III, 167–70)

That could be a marginal gloss for Marlowe's twenty lines, which constitute three fairly symmetrical strophes. The starting point for the first, the invocation, is the most rhetorical of questions. Though it is Marlowe's culminating hyperbole, it may not strike us with the fullest impact, precisely because it has struck so often before, because it has been echoed and reëchoed as one of the striking exaggerations of poetry—like the tower of ivory in the Song of Songs. The thousand ships are not exaggerated; they are specified by Ovid's matter-of-fact account of the Trojan War in the *Metamorphoses* (XII, 7); but here poetic audacity intervenes to transpose a lover's emotion into a large-scale naval operation. The topless towers are recurrent symbols for illimitable aspiration, and Marlowe habitually juxtaposes them to the all-consuming element of fire. Cavalierly he poses a moral issue, and the alternative is absolute: the destruction of a city, the calamities of war, the world well lost, all for love.

> Was this the face that lancht a thousand shippes?
> And burnt the toplesse Towres of *Ilium*?
> Sweete *Helen,* make me immortall with a kisse.
>
>   (1328–30)

The third line is an implicit stage direction, leading on to the enactment of a metaphysical conceit; whereupon Faustus claims that Helen's lips suck forth his soul, and then reclaims it with another kiss. Underneath their amorous byplay runs the disturbing hint that she may be a succuba; this may not be the only world that is at stake for him. When Dido wooed Æneas and spoke of becoming "immortall with a kisse" (1329), it seemed to be little more than a figure of speech. For Faustus immortality means vastly more than that, in one way if not in another, although he may actually get no closer to heaven than Helen's embrace. No wonder he changes his evaluation from other-worldly to mercenary terms:

> Here wil I dwel, for heauen be in these lips,
> And all is drosse that is not *Helena.* (1333-4)

The second strophe is in the active mode of *Tamburlaine,* and the phrase "I wil" resounds through it. Since Helen is notoriously a *casus belli,* Faustus proposes to reënact the Trojan War through the sack of Wittenberg. He will be Paris as, in parody, Ithamore would be Jason, with Bellamira for his golden fleece. Faustus challenges the Greek heroes to a tournament, imagined as medieval tapestry rather than a classical frieze, a colorful but two-dimensional representation of the basic conflict between pagan and Christian values. In the third strophe the knight, returning to the lady he has championed, salutes her with a gallant array of invidious comparisons and mythological superlatives. He modulates from the threat to the persuasion, the more passive mode of *Edward II.* If he cannot visualize Helen distinctly, it is because she bedazzles him. Her fairness, outshining the starlight, surpasses the goddesses—or is it the gods?

> Brighter art thou then flaming *Iupter,*
> When he appeard to haplesse *Semele,*
> More louely then the monarke of the skie
> In wanton *Arethusaes* azurde armes.
>
> (1343-6)

It is not to these nymphs, but to Jupiter himself, that Helen is being compared. Strange as this may seem, it is not inconsistent with the prologue's allusion to a masculine muse. It throws some light back on the offer of Mephostophilis to procure the fairest of women for Faustus, be they as chaste as Penelope, as wise as the Queen of Sheba,

> or as beautiful
> As was bright *Lucifer* before his fall.
> (589-90)

Helen, whatever she is, whoever she was, says nothing. Her part is purely visual, entirely mute. Faustus might almost be talking to himself, and when we notice how many of his speeches are addressed to himself, the play becomes a kind of interior monologue. Whatever satisfaction he obtains from Helen is bound to be illusory; as a necro-

mancer he knows in advance that the shadow is not substantial, that
the apparition he has materialized will vanish sooner or later. The
Faustbook reports that she bore him a child, which disappeared—
along with its mother—on the day of Faustus' death. Was it a vision
or a waking dream, or does the fair exterior disguise some hideous
monster like Keats's Lamia? Lucian, in his *Dialogues of the Dead*,
pictures Menippus descending into the underworld, inquiring after
Helen, and being shown a skeleton. Yes, Hermes assures him, this was
the skull that caused the Greeks to launch a thousand ships. And
the refrain is the timeless *Ubi sunt?* Where are they now—Helen,
Thaïs, Dido, Zenocrate? Marlowe cannot have been insensitive to the
traditional mood so poignantly expressed by his sometime collaborator, Thomas Nashe:

> Brightnesse falls from the ayre,
> Queenes have died yong and faire,
> Dust hath closde Helens eye . . .

It is not for nothing that Faustus characterizes Helen by her face,
with the connotation of skin-deep beauty as opposed to harsh truth.
His rhetoric is an ornate façade, an esthetic surface masking an ethi-
cal reality. A third dimension is given to the speech by the entrance
—after the first strophe—of a third character, who is indubitably
real. This is the Old Man, whom the *Faustbook* identifies as a neigh-
bor, the exemplary figure whom Marlowe employs as a spokesman for
Christianity and a counterweight for the ideal of paganism. It is he
who penetrates Faustus' conscience:

> Breake heart, drop bloud, and mingle it with teares.

> (1277)

Faustus admits his sinfulness and might be moved to repent, were
it not for the threatening Mephostophilis and the enticing Helen.
When Faustus sweeps her off the stage, it is the Old Man who stays
to pronounce the moral; and while Faustus enjoys her elusive favors,
the Old Man is "sifted" and tried by devils; but his faith triumphs
over Satan's pride, and he ascends to heaven while the fiends sink back
into hell. The absence of this crucial speech is a reason for continuing
to distrust the 1616 Quarto.

With every scene the pace of the drama accelerates, reaching a
climax with the final monologue, which syncopates an hour into fifty-
nine lines. This is much too fast, and we share the suspense with
Faustus, whose contract expires at midnight; and yet, in a sense, it is
slow enough to fathom—as it were—the thoughts of a drowning man.
It is a soliloquy in the profoundest sense, since it isolates the speaker;

at the end, as at the beginning, we find him alone in his study. Tragedy is an isolating experience. To each of us, as to Proust on the death of his grandmother, it conveys the realization that we are truly alone. When the time comes, each tragic protagonist must say, with Shakespeare's Juliet:

> My dismall Sceane, I needs must act alone.
>
> (IV, iii, 19)

So with Faustus, whose fellow scholars rally him for becoming "ouer solitary" (1363). They must leave him to his solitude, just as the friends of Everyman desert him on his way to the grave. In contradistinction to the specious grandeur of Faustus' apostrophe to Helen, his last words are an inner revelation, the excruciated agony of a lost soul. It is now too late for vaunting or pleading; it is Marlowe's occasion to develop the less characteristic mode of lamentation; and he does so with the utmost resourcefulness, timing and complicating his flexible rhythms to catch the agitations of Faustus' tortured mind. It is hard to think of another single speech, even in Shakespeare, which demands more from the actor or offers him more. Edward Alleyn, in a surplice with a cross upon it, was famed for his portrayal of the part and may well have left some marks upon these lines. They begin, with a portentous sound effect, at the stroke of eleven:

> Ah Faustus,
> Now hast thou but one bare hower to liue,
> And then thou must be damnd perpetually.
>
> (1419–21)

Time is the essence, and also the substance, of the soliloquy. Its underlying contrast between eternity and transience is heavily enforced, in this distich, by a slow succession of monosyllables leading up to the rapid adverb, with the hypermetrical syllable, "perpetually." Words of comparable significance—"ever," "still," "forever," "everlasting"—abound throughout. Where Edward implored the sun to gallop apace and hasten events, Faustus now bids the planetary system stand still. A humanist to the last, he recalls a line from Ovid's *Elegies*:

> *O lente, lente curite noctis equi.*
>
> (1428)

The utterance falls ironically, but not inappropriately, from the lips of the scholar turned sensualist, the erstwhile lover of Helen of Troy. The difference is vast between his motive for wanting the dawn to be postponed and the classical lover's plea to Aurora. As Marlowe himself had rendered it:

Now in her tender armes I sweetly bide,
If euer, now well lies she by my side.
The aire is cold, and sleepe is sweetest now
And birdes send forth shrill notes from euery bough:
Whither runst thou, that men, and women loue not?
Hold in thy rosy horses that they moue not . . .
But heldst thou in thine armes some *Cephalus,*
Then wouldst thou cry, stay night and runne not thus.

(I, xiii, 5–40)

Such a miracle might be accomplished at the behest of the gods, as Jupiter boasted in *Dido;* but for Faustus, all too human, the spheres go on revolving. Soon it will be his turn to be tormented; and he is not armed, as the Old Man was, with faith. Suddenly he seems to witness an epiphany. "See see," he exclaims, "where Christs blood streames in the firmament" (1432). The line echoes and answers Tamburlaine's final challenge, when he threatened to march against the powers of heaven and "set blacke streamers in the firmament." The change of colors is emblematic of two opposing attitudes toward death: massacre for the man of war, sacrifice for the man of peace. When Faustus excommunicated himself by signing the deed, his own blood was ominously reluctant to flow. He asked, "Why streames it not?" (498) and coals were brought to warm it—more omens. Blood, for the Guise, was the only fluid that could extinguish the flames of lawless ambition; but Faustus is denied the blood of Christ, the only thing that could save him, because of his own denial. "The heauy wrath of God" (1439), as the Good Angel admonished, is now on his head; and his diction grows scriptural, echoing the Prophets and the Apocalypse, as he vainly thinks of hiding from the "irefull browes" of Jehovah. The striking of the half-hour alerts him again to temporal considerations, both relative and absolute.

O no end is limited to damned soules.

(1458)

Damnation is an unlooked-for way of transcending limits and approaching infinity; it is immortality with a vengeance; and Faustus would rather be a soulless beast and look forward to oblivion. Marlowe elsewhere uses the trope of "water drops" when he reckons innumerable quantities. Here, with fire in the offing, they are a welcome mirage of dissolution; now, from the combining elements, a vapor ascends. If time oscillates between swiftness and slowness, space is measured by the span between heaven and hell. Although those two words are paired off against each other in this speech and through the play, somehow "hell" and its cognates occur fifty-eight times to forty-nine occurrences for "heaven"—the proportion is forty-five to twenty-seven in the shorter edition. Faustus is accorded a glimpse of paradise in the *Faustbook*; the 1616 Quarto directs the "throne," the Elizabethan god-in-the-machine, briefly to descend from the "heavens," the roof of the stage; while hell, which is also conveniently adjacent to the localities of the play, yawns in a discovery scene. The denouement is a foregone conclusion: "for vaine pleasure of 24. yeares hath Faustus lost eternall ioy and felicitie" (1396).

As the clock strikes twelve, with thunder and lightning, the leaping demons enter to carry him off; in terror he makes his last offer to burn his books, and his very last word is the shriek, *"Mephostophilis."* He makes his definitive exit through the monstrous jaws of the hell-mouth. That popular but obsolete property, which Marlowe resurrected from the mysteries, symbolizes pain and punishment more terribly than the sordid details of Edward's murder and more pitifully than the crude melodrama of Barabas' caldron. There is one more scene in the 1616 version, where the scholars interchange proper moral sentiments; like the sextet at the end of *Don Giovanni,* it seems unduly sententious after what has just happened; and, with some justification, it is not printed in the Quarto of 1604. The Chorus, or Wagner, draws the arras across the inner stage, and the black curtain prevails over the smoking red grotesquerie. If the classical imagery of the epilogue is at odds with its medieval purport, this reflects the tension of the play. If the branch is cut, if Apollo's laurel is burnt, let it be an object lesson for those "forward wits" who are so enticed by "deepnesse." The celestial-infernal antithesis is conclusively asserted, and the workings of "heauenly power" are discerned in the "hellish fall" of Dr. Faustus. Thus the tragedy is framed by the fundamental dogmas of Christian morality. How far, then, should they be taken literally? How far do they merely furnish Marlowe with expressionistic scenery? How far was he utilizing theology as a modern playwright might utilize psychology? Faustus has maintained that hell is a fable, and Mephostophilis has declared— in an unexpected burst of humanistic fervor—that man is more excellent than heaven. Dr. Faustus' worst mistake has been to confound hell with Elysium. Between the classic shades and the quenchless flames, even in *Tamburlaine,* Marlowe had discriminated. If heaven was placed in hell, or hell in heaven, the inversion had to be reversed; and the reversal is all the more decisive in *Doctor Faustus* because it comes as a recognition, and because the movement of Marlowe's imagination—at its uppermost—turns and takes a plunge into the abyss.

Unless, with the credulous members of his audience, we regard his fireworks as sparks of hellfire, we must assume that Marlowe's Inferno is a genuine but unlocalized phenomenon. In the same spirit, Para-

celsus repeatedly averred that there is a heaven in each of us, and
Milton's Satan announces: "My self am Hell" (IV, 75). There is a god
infused through the universe, so it was affirmed in *Tamburlaine*; and
there is a hell which has no limits, Faustus is informed by Mephostophilis. Every man, according to his lights and through his own
endeavors, has a chance to know both; and Milton is not being
paradoxical when Satan announces in *Paradise Lost*:

> The mind is its own place, and in it self
> Can make a Heav'n of Hell, a Hell of Heav'n.
>
> (I, 254-55)

The Seven Deadly Sins, the Good and Evil Angels, Mephostophilis
himself, upon this level, may be regarded as materializations like Helen
of Troy. "Hell striues with grace" in a *psychomachia*, a spiritual battle
within the breast of Faustus (1302). Pointedly the Old Man rebukes
him for excluding "the grace of heauen" from his soul (1349). It is
plainly lacking, but has he excluded it? Before his blood was dry on
the parchment, he was thoroughly remorseful; and his remorse, increasing over his pleasure, gradually deepens into the hopeless despair
of his concluding soliloquy.

> Contrition, prayer, repentance: what of them?
>
> (448)

he has wondered; he has resolved to renounce his magic, and been
distracted by his Evil Angel. Later, when his Good Angel all but
persuades him to repent, he tries; but his heart is so hardened that
he can scarcely utter such words as "saluation, faith, or heauen" (630).
Yet he does so, with no little eloquence; and, by uttering the name of
God, he prays—albeit no more effectually than Claudius in *Hamlet*.
As between the "Neuer too late" of the Good Angel and the "Too late"
of the Evil Angel, the latter prevails with a Manichæan fatality (691).
Christian doctrine vouchsafes mercy to repentant sinners:

> Tush, Christ did call the thiefe vpon the Crosse.
>
> (1147)

Even "the Serpent that tempted *Eue* may be sau'd" (1371). Then why
not Faustus? Having become a spirit in form and substance, has he
ceased to be a man? Why, when the Old Man all but converts him,
should Faustus accept the dagger of Mephostophilis? Why, when he
calls upon Christ, is it Lucifer who emerges? George Santayana, acting
as devil's advocate, and felicitously stating the case for Faustus as a
martyr to the ideals of the Renaissance, would argue that he "is
damned by accident or by predestination; he is browbeaten by the

devil and forbidden to repent when he has really repented." The pedestrian counterargument would be based on the *Faustbook's* account of Faustus, "neuer falling to repentance truly" but "in all his opinions doubtfull, without faith or hope." Luther, followed by such English theologians as Richard Hooker, in his revolt against Catholicism had made contrition so difficult that at times it seemed virtually unattainable. What was worse for Faustus, he was no ordinary sinner; he was, like Marlowe himself, that impenitent and willful miscreant whom Elizabethan preachers termed a scorner. Far from denying sin or its wages, death, his course of action was premised on their inevitability: *Che sera, sera.* This led him, not to fatalism, but to an extreme act of the will—namely, the commission of an unpardonable sin, a sin against the Holy Ghost. Casuistry could have found theological loopholes, had a penitent Faustus been conceivable. But that would have presupposed an orthodox Marlowe.

Marlowe's *Doctor Faustus:*
The Repudiation of Humanity

by Roland M. Frye

On many counts Marlowe's *Doctor Faustus* may stand as a prime example in Elizabethan drama of what Sir Philip Sidney applauded as "that feigning notable images of virtues, vices, or what else, with that delightful teaching, which must be the right describing note to know a poet by." Since Sidney died in 1586, it is highly improbable that he had seen *Doctor Faustus,* and it is perhaps as well that he had not, for in it Marlowe violates all of Sidney's technical standards for the well-made play even while demonstrating allegiance to Sidney's moral imperatives. Matching "hornpipes and funerals," "mingling kings and clowns," Marlowe totally ignores the dictum that "the stage should always represent but one place, and the uttermost time . . . but one day." Instead of twenty-four hours, Marlowe's action covers twenty-four years, and the place is restricted only to Europe, though Hell, too, plays an important and ever encroaching role upon the scene. Despite these violations of unity in the conventional sense, Marlowe's play remains a unified drama in its major dimensions of character and plot and in this way presents what Sidney fundamentally desired in an imitation of life which simultaneously teaches and delights. Indeed, in *Faustus* there is no plot apart from character, no plot apart from what Faustus himself says, thinks, feels, and does. Here character and plot are so completely integrated that neither is possible without the other, and the two so interconnect as to explain, justify, and complete each the other.

The coming of Mephistophilis is an apt example of this integration, for his appearance is explicitly described as a response to character rather than to action. In reply to Faustus's question as to the effect of the conjuring act, Mephistophilis replies that it was the cause "but yet *per accidens,*" the real cause being Faustus's demonstration that

---

"Marlowe's Doctor Faustus: *The Repudiation of Humanity" by Roland M. Frye,* South Atlantic Quarterly, *Vol. LV, No. 3 (July, 1956), 322–28. Copyright © 1956 by Duke University Press. Reprinted by permission of the publisher.*

he was "in danger to be damned." Mephistophilis's appearance, then, is clearly in response to the blasphemy of Faustus, which in turn springs from Faustus's repudiation of humanity "to gain a deity." The original sin of Faustus is the original sin of man, the abandonment of the image of God in order to be as God, in Eve's terms, or, as Faustus puts it, to "be on earth as Jove is in the sky."

The desire for knowledge was involved, to be sure, but the desire was not for knowledge in the natural sense, for Faustus already possessed such knowledge to a final degree ("Is not thy common talk sound aphorisms?"). The knowledge desired here is the knowledge with which the serpent tempted Eve, the knowledge which would make man more than human. As for natural knowledge, we do not see Faustus achieving it by his bargain, for Mephistophilis's answers to his questions are but "freshmen's suppositions" which even Wagner could decide. The only knowledge which Faustus achieves—and the only power through knowledge—is of the chimerical, of phantasms, of false shows and masquerades. To the Emperor he admits that he cannot present "true substantial bodies" but only "spirits as can lively resemble."

Not only does this restriction apply to the presentation of Alexander and "his beauteous paramour," but also to the very Helen who comes in response to Faustus's final prayer. The answer to the lovely lines

> Was this the face that launched a thousand ships,
> And burnt the topless towers of Ilium?

is, inevitably, "no," and this never enunciated "no" constitutes a major dramatic irony in the play. The same irony underlies the beautiful appeal "Sweet Helen, make me immortal with a kiss," for this *is* an immortal kiss, as "her lips," says Faustus, "suck forth my soul."

But that particular immortality awarded to Faustus comes not primarily as the result of sensuality, though that was surely involved as early as the first meeting with Mephistophilis, when Faustus demanded to live "in all voluptuousness." Again, at the end, after the second blood pact, Faustus prays the magnificently piercing prayer that he be given Helen "to glut the longing of my heart's desire." So it is with a demon disguised

> fairer than the evening air
> Clad in the beauty of a thousand stars

that Faustus ultimately extinguishes clean "these thoughts that do dissuade me from my vow, . . . mine oath I made to Lucifer."

All this is procedent from the basic rejection and does not constitute the original sin, which was usurpation upon deity. Though

surely a part of Faustus's admitted "surfeit of deadly sin," sensual delight was not its root. Marlowe's presentation of sin is purer, more
central, than that. Like Calvin, although not necessarily after him,
he does not consider the ultimate evil in merely prurient and periph-
eral terms. So Calvin calls it "a fond and foolish thing," and a mark of
gross ignorance, to see original sin in terms of "the sensual motions"
or to restrict it to what is called sensuality. The sensuality was a later
development—perhaps, as Marlowe's words may suggest, to "glut the
longing" of a heart which has revolted from its true uses—but the
basic evil may be seen in Calvin's terms which parallel Marlowe's
conception, that this "son of earth thought it a small thing that he was
made after the likeness of God, unless he might also be made equal
with God."

This, as I suggest, is a particularly pure, unembarrassed, and central
view of sin—sin in the ultimate and basic dimension as usurpation
upon the deity and repudiation of humanity. Faustus's relation to the
deity is through envy and cupidity, not through charity. His imitation
of God is as a rival, and his preoccupation with the ascension above
humanity ("Yet art thou still but Faustus, and a man") results in the
irrevoked repudiation of the *imago dei* in favor of what Faustus calls
"Mephistophilis fratris imagine." From this all else stems, whether in
character or in action.

The new world of Faustus, the world in which he exists as "Lord
and commander," is a world of illusion and of buffoonery. The great
intellect who was wont to make the Protestant university of Wittenberg ring with *sic probo* is reduced to a buffooning, slapstick assault
upon the Pope and his court in a most degrading and ridiculous
spectacle. To be sure, much of the central portion of the play has
impressed critics as being unlike Marlowe and as being at least in
part spurious; even so, it is nonetheless meaningfully inserted. In the
very degradation of the horseplay scenes we may confront the tragedy
of Faustus. Upon the first appearance of Mephistophilis, Faustus had
indicated his rejection of reality in the refusal to accept the demonic
in its true revelation:

> I charge thee to return, and change thy shape;
> Thou art too ugly to attend on me:
> Go, and return an old Franciscan friar;
> That holy shape becomes a devil best.

From this point onward Faustus's hold upon reality steadily dissolves,
and the debasing horseplay—first with the Pope, later with the honest
knight, and then with the poor courser—serves to underscore the
dissolution of Faustus's human dignity. Even the conjuring games of

the low-life characters point by parallelism to the pettiness of Faustus's accomplishments.

Reality is for Faustus no longer determinative. He has rejected creation in favor of chaos, for only thus could he maintain the services of Mephistophilis. "Think thou on hell, Faustus, for thou art damned," says Mephistophilis, and the aroused Lucifer commands that he

> Talk not of Paradise nor creation; but mark this show:
> talk of the devil, and nothing else.

So Faustus, having rejected God and his own creatureliness, must now reject creation too, and the quality of his own existence becomes determined by the norm of chaos. It is within this context that the seemingly indiscriminate hurly-burly of the central scenes become meaningful embodiments, whether by Marlowe or another, of Faustus's reintroduction of chaos.

The very fact of Faustus's fame is environed with buffoonery, and this is quite proper. Indeed, his position is but small remove from that of a wandering juggler, entertaining various courts with his shows and entertaining himself with largely irresponsible pranks. How far removed is this realization from his earlier hopes! It was his desire to do great things, to

> chase the Prince of Parma from our land,
> And reign sole king of all our provinces.

Again, "the signiory of Emden shall be mine," and

> The Emp'ror shall not live but by my leave,
> Nor any potentate of Germany.

Instead, though feasted with the noblemen, he finds himself employed as an entertainer to the Emperor whom he had earlier hoped to control, and finds himself pensioned off at the conclusion of the evening's show. The spirits whom he hoped to see drag huge argosies from Venice and "from America the golden fleece" do manage to present the pregnant Duchess of Vanholt with a bunch of grapes, but this marks the extent of their transportation, and beyond this range Faustus's power scarcely seems to extend. Again, Faustus accepts the patronage of those whom he once had hoped to patronize. Such sustained contrasts between the plot which Faustus gets and the plot which he had envisioned for his life constitute another of the effective ironies of the tragedy. The demands for knowledge and for power finally cease, and the last request is for Helen—the demon-lover—who becomes an existential symbol for the repudiation of creation and for Faustus's "marriage" with hell.

Like this final union, the two blood pacts forcefully embody the significance of a total existential dedication. There is melodrama here, of course, but there is more than that, for it is symbolically essential that Faustus's commitment to hell should be signed *with* his life, *with* his most intimate being. At the first pact, his very blood protests, but not at the second pact. There is meaning in this difference, for much has happened in twenty-four years. The Good Angel has appeared to Faustus four times, all told, to urge repentance and return. The last time Faustus sees the Good Angel is before the appearance of the aroused Lucifer, who proscribes all thoughts of creation. Beyond this point, Faustus cannot again either see or hear the direct messenger of heaven. His heart is hardening, he later admits, and his only hope is presumption ("Tush, Christ did call the thief upon the cross"), but that there is still hope until the time of the second blood bond and the demonic consummation with Helen there can be no doubt. Indeed, the Old Man's primary function is to indicate that Faustus still can "call for mercy, and avoid despair," and he mediates to Faustus the vision of grace which Faustus himself can no longer directly see:

> Ah, stay, good Faustus, stay thy desperate steps!
> I see an angel hovers o'er thy head,
> And, with a vial full of precious grace,
> Offers to pour the same into thy soul.

But this vision Faustus now rejects in the ultimate rejection, and seeks his pardon from Lucifer rather than from God. Thus, as the sorely afflicted Old Man says, Faustus excludes the grace of heaven from his soul and so seals the unforgivable sin against the Holy Ghost.

The final catastrophe is presented with the swift, deft marks of dramatic genius. The drama closes, as it opens, with Faustus significantly alone. The prelude to the close is in Faustus's cry of anguish to his friends that he "must remain in hell for ever—hell, ah, hell, for ever! Sweet friends, what shall become of Faustus, being in hell for ever?" And then the scholars leave, and he is alone, his life come full circle. He desires escape—not for the love of God but for the fear of hell—and, caught up in the final tension and anguish of the striking clock which counts out the moments of remaining life, he once more explicitly and feverishly repudiates his humanity. But, whereas in the beginning his discontentment was in that "yet art thou still but Faustus, and a man," and his impelling desire was "to gain a deity," to be on earth "as Jove is in the sky," he now finally rejects humanity in favor of an opposite extreme. He would now repudiate his immortality, would be changed

> Unto some brutish beast! all beasts are happy,
> For, when they die,
> Their souls are soon dissolved in elements.

But such a repudiation is not sufficiently radical to express the ulti-mate terror which grips Faustus's soul as he rushes on to reject not only reason and immortality but even the most basic sentience, even animation itself:

> O soul, be chang'd into little water-drops,
> And fall into the ocean, ne'er be found!

As the character Faustus thus utterly repudiates his existence, the demons come, and the plot of *Faustus* is closed. A devil enters, and Faustus cries out against him—now seen in all the terrifying ugliness which has so long been concealed—"My God, my God, look not so fierce on me," and the rest is the eternal death for which he had bargained.

The rejection of humanity which constituted the character of Faustus is complete, and the plot closes, as it had opened, with this. It is in these terms that Marlowe achieves unity and by virtue of this unity that he has rendered aesthetically powerful an understanding of the human condition which has never been more central to the plight of man than it is in our own time. Albert Schweitzer, in his acceptance speech for the Nobel Peace Prize, put it in these terms: "The super-man, in the measure that his power increases, becomes himself poorer and poorer. . . . The more we become supermen, the more we become inhuman."

The Vision of Tragedy in *Doctor Faustus*

by Richard B. Sewall

W. H. Auden observed that at the end of a Greek tragedy we say, "What a pity it had to be this way"; at the end of a Christian tragedy, "What a pity it had to be this way when it might have been otherwise." [1] If there is more freedom in Greek tragedy and more of a sense of fate in Christian tragedy than this statement suggests, still it points to the true tragic locus and tone of Marlowe's *Doctor Faustus,* the first major Elizabethan tragedy and the first to explore the tragic possibilities of the head-on clash of the Renaissance compulsions with the Hebraic-Christian tradition. His *Tamburlaine,* presumably written in the previous year (1587), for all its scenes of violence and pathos, was more of a single-voiced statement of the outward Renaissance thrust, a reckless flouting, without much inner concern, of all that Greeks knew as *hubris* and fate and all that Christians knew as sin, guilt, and damnation. Marlowe viewed it as "tragic," perhaps, in its picture of suffering and destruction and in the spectacle of death overtaking in the end even this mightiest of worldly conquerors.[2] Al-

---

"*The Vision of Tragedy in* Doctor Faustus" *(Editor's title). From* The Vision of Tragedy *by Richard B. Sewall (New Haven: Yale University Press, 1959), pp. 57–67, 159–60. Copyright © 1959 by Yale University Press. Reprinted by permission of the publisher.*

[1] "The Christian Tragic Hero," *New York Times Book Review,* Dec. 16, 1945. I agree with Laurence Michel . . . that tragedy is not Christian and never can be, and that such terms as "Christian tragedy" involve dangerous ambiguities. But (to repeat): the term is permissible and, I think, useful, to indicate the new dimensions and tensions introduced into human life by Christianity and which perforce entered into the Elizabethan tragic synthesis. Tragedy puts to the test *all* the formulations of a culture and comes out committed to none. What Auden describes as the Greek "tragedy of necessity" actually shows the extent to which man is free in the midst of fate; and what he calls the Christian "tragedy of possibility" shows the old sense of fate in the midst of the new freedom. I use this much-quoted remark from his *New York Times* essay merely to point to the central stress (not new but more exigent) of Elizabethan tragedy.

[2] Cf. Theodore Spencer, *Death and Elizabethan Tragedy* (Cambridge, Harvard University Press, 1936), p. 232. To the Elizabethans, "Death, indeed, *was* tragedy; a tragedy was a play which ended in death." Death was feared as "the end of accomplishment"; it destroyed beauty, power, wealth—all the good things of life. Spencer suggests (to anticipate for a moment) that the increasing number of

though there are spiritual reaches and broodings in *Tamburlaine* that Marlowe never got from the Greeks, it was in *Faustus* that he turned the focus inward, saw the soul as the tragic battlefield, and wrote the first "Christian tragedy."

"Cut is the branch that might have grown full straight." So says the Chorus in the final speech of *Faustus,* bringing the play to a typical morality-play or *De Casibus*-story ending with a warning against such fiendish practices as Faustus followed. "What a pity it had to be this way when it might have been otherwise." The choice which would have made all the difference belonged to Faustus, and he knew it. No god urged him on, no oracle foretold his fate. He sinned, suffered remorse, and was damned. The medieval predecessors of the play had told the same story, with variations, again and again; and insofar as *Faustus* merely repeats the old pattern it is anything but tragic. There is no mystery in this kind of universe; it is all too predictable, and the moral issues are clear cut. The terror, had Faustus only chosen differently, might have been avoided; and we are left comfortable and secure in the knowledge of how to escape his downfall.

But Marlowe did not merely repeat the old pattern, and his universe is not comfortable or secure. The Elizabethan theater invited something like the same kind of aesthetic interest in the direful aspects of human experience that Greek tragedy had stimulated in both artist and spectator. Indeed, knowledge of the Greek form, to humanists like Marlowe, must have had a compulsive force of its own, quite apart from personal predilections—although in Marlowe's case, there is evidence that those predilections were many and strong. That the Greeks had once ordered and presented human experience in such a way, and so powerfully, was an inescapable and compelling fact. Popular taste, which had been nourished on the rudimentary action of the old religious (but increasingly secular) plays, asked to see the full story acted out. With the dramatic treatment of action freed from ecclesiastical control, the way was open for the expression once again of "tragic" truth—the truth of man in action as seen by the free and inquiring artist. Marlowe had said enough in *Tamburlaine* to get himself excommunicated many times over, but he had said it in a play, in a dramatic context, and he was not prevented from writing more plays. If, in *Faustus,* he brings the play to a pious conclusion, the

tragedies during the early years of the seventeenth century was due in part, at least, to a kind of national preoccupation with death during Elizabeth's last years and following her death. "There is more than merely biographical importance in the fact that Shakespeare stopped writing comedies in [these years]. He simply expressed better than anyone else the trend of contemporary thought. . . . He began to contemplate life tragically" (p. 233). (One is reminded of Dr. Johnson's remark [19 Sept. 1777]: "Depend upon it, Sir, when a man knows he is to be hanged in a fortnight, it concentrates his mind wonderfully.")

"truth" of the play goes far beyond the Chorus' final piety, just as the meaning of *Oedipus* transcends by far the choric summing up of that play. The voice of the Chorus is not the only voice in *Faustus*. For one thing, no figure of the old moralities talks so much or takes us so deep into his own being as does Faustus—or does so much and so boldly. Faustus in thought and action, brooding, philosophizing, disputing, conjuring, defying God and risking all with a flourish, does not suggest so much the lay figure of the moralities, Everyman, as, (in one of his phases) Adam the knowledge-seeker and (in others) the defiant hero of the Greek tradition—a Prometheus or Tamburlaine.

Thus the "secret cause," the true source of the tragic terror of the story of *Faustus* as Marlowe treated it, does not lie in the Christian moral equation of which Faustus in the end finds himself an inevitable term. The "fearful echoes" that "thunder in his ears" in the interludes between his conjuring exploits are momentarily terrifying to him but not because of the mystery of their origin, which is fifteen centuries of Christian teaching and spiritual discipline. He tells the Scholars (Scene 14) that he suffers from "a surfeit of deadly sin that hath damned both body and soul." Such was the fate of the sixteenth-century German magician whose story Marlowe dramatized. But like the Poet of Job and the Greek tragedians, who found new and tragic meaning in old and orthodox stories, Marlowe interpolated into the old medieval equation the new, mysterious, and terrifyingly ambiguous dynamic of the Renaissance, gave it a fascination and a dignity never realized in previous treatments of the story, and made Faustus, rather than Hamlet, "the first modern man." The story of this twenty-four-year action, telescoped by Marlowe into a few vivid scenes, introduced the modern tragic theme of the divided soul—soon to become "the complicated modern soul" of Dostoevski's analysis—torn between the desire to exploit its new mastery and freedom and (on the other hand) the claims of the old teachings, which to defy meant guilt and a growing sense of alienation. Faustus is tragic because he recognized the dilemma as real. Even as he boasts that his soul is his own, to dispose of as he will, he hears the fearful echoes thundering in his ears.

As with Job and Oedipus, we first see Faustus at the peak of his worldly power and influence. He is master of the new knowledges and skills, a famous physician, honored by whole cities, and revered by his students. Why was he restless? Why was he unwilling to remain "but Faustus, and a man"? Why this urge to command "all things that move between the quiet poles"? "The one fixed star" of tragedy, writes Arthur Miller,[3] is the hero's urge to "realize himself" fully in the face

---

[3] "Tragedy and the Common Man," *New York Times Theater Section*, Feb. 27, 1949. Miller here stresses what I regard as only the first phase of the tragic hero's experience, the romantic or rebellious phase: Faustus, that is, as he embarks on his course.

of all that would rob him of his just deserts or repress what he feels to be his true nature; and the gauge of his heroism is the magnitude of the risk he is willing to take. In this sense the tragedy of Faustus is the tragedy of Adam, "goaded" (as Kierkegaard saw it) by the knowledge of his freedom into what seemed like the one possibility of self-realization his situation offered. Paradise was not enough. To the orthodox, Adam's action was not only sin but utter folly, just as to the Chorus who begins and ends the play Faustus' action was wholly devilish. This too is the sense of the opening soliloquy, in which Faustus brushes aside all studies but necromancy, the key to the self-realization he craves. Immediately the Good Angel tells him to "lay that damned book aside," and the Angel who bids him "go forward in that famous art" is "Evil."

But to Marlowe (judging from the way he presented it) the case was more complicated and more fascinating. He saw the entire action not only as "Good" or "Evil" would see it but as the man of flesh and blood, the one who takes the risk, sees it and lives it out. What are the inner sources of such an action, what is the feel on the pulse, what is the discovery? The meaning of the play is not only that Faustus' act was sinful and foolish. The meaning is in all that Faustus says and does and becomes; it is the total yield of the "boundary-situation" into which Faustus walks of his own accord, acting out the mysterious tragic dynamic of his times.

If Job began in bitterness, and Oedipus in self-confidence too close to complacence, Faustus' first mood after seizing upon necromancy as his study is one of arrogant and impatient lust for power. It is redeemed, if at all, by the full imaginative run that gives even his petty wishes—"the pleasant fruits and princely delicates"—a kind of poetic validity. Marlowe sets his hero's mind completely free to range forbidden realms, and no voice save Tamburlaine's gives comparable expression to the outward Renaissance thrust.

> All things that move between the quiet poles
> Shall be at my command. Emperors and kings
> Are but obeyed in their several provinces,
> Nor can they raise the wind or rend the clouds;
> But his dominion that exceeds in this
> Stretcheth as far as doth the mind of man.
> A sound magician is a mighty god:
> Here, Faustus, try thy brains to gain a deity!

"How am I glutted with conceit of this!" cries Faustus, as he relishes his promised power over all things great and little, temporal and spiritual. His whirling wishes at first have little pattern, no redeeming cause or ideal—no quest for justice or truth; and as his desires grow

more fantastic and vain-glorious the spectacle is not pretty. But the
opening scenes do not wholly condemn him. His absurd egotisms are
mixed with intellectual and humanitarian impulses. He would "re-
solve all ambiguities," read strange philosophy, clothe the schoolboys
in silk, and rid his country of the foreign yoke. When Valdes warns
him that he must be "resolute," his courage is tested and he responds
like a hero. He is prepared (at the end of Scene 1) to take the ultimate
risk: "This night I'll conjure though I die therefore." Later, in Scene
3, he rallies the spirits of the Devil's own messenger, Mephistophilis,
whose heart faints as he foresees Faustus' awful future. Rising in his
"manly fortitude," he scorns Mephistophilis' warning, rejects all hopes
of heaven's joys, and offers his soul to Lucifer for twenty-four years of
his heart's desires. With his decision come new energy, new power,
new command. However "evil" his course, he has left the apathetic and
cynical talk of the opening lines of the play and is now man "on the
way."

It is said that the great tragedies deal with the great eccentrics and
offenders, the God-defiers, the murderers, the adulterers. But it is not
tragedy's primary concern to establish the moral truth or the sociological meaning of the hero's action. It is the orthodox world, and not the
tragic artist, which judges (or prejudges) a Job or an Oedpius, a
Faustus or a Hester Prynne. To bring his protagonist swiftly to the
point of ultimate test, the artist imagines a deed which violently
challenges the accepted social and (it may be) legal ways. Hence the
fact that tragic heroes are often criminals in the eyes of society, and
hence the frequency of the legal trial as a symbolic situation in
tragedy from Aeschylus to Dostoevski and Kafka. It is the characteristic
emphasis of tragedy written in the Christian era that the "criminals"
become "sinners" as well, so that the hero is ranged not only against
his society but against God and his own soul. Starbuck could not see
why Ahab should go whaling for anything but profit; he was aghast
at Ahab's "sin" toward one of God's dumb creatures; and had the
Pequod ever returned, Ahab would have had to stand trial for his
criminal neglect of his charge, as before Starbuck's God he must stand
trial for his immortal soul. But *Moby-Dick* is not primarily concerned
with Ahab as a criminal or sinner, nor is Marlowe's play primarily
concerned with Faustus as the Church or society would regard him.
The moral qualities or the sociological aspects of the hero's initial
choice are less important than the qualities he shows and the dis-
coveries he makes in the subsequent action. Indeed, as Dostoevski
was to show about the increasingly standardized society of his time, for
purposes of moral discovery the "criminals and outcasts" provide the
richest material for the inquiring artist. Judged in this scale, it was
better for Faustus to sell his soul, for Hester to sin with Dimmesdale,

and for Raskolnikov to commit murder than that no action at all be joined. Thus (as we have seen) the Greeks respected pride and made it a heroic quality, though they saw its destructive side. Stripped of its eschatology, the Christian doctrine of the *felix culpa,* the fortunate fall of Adam, is akin to the treatment in tragedy of the hero's initial crime or sin.[4] Precarious as such an ethic is, tragedy holds aloof from moral judgment and presents the action in such a way that moral judgment can be only one element, and not the most important, in the total response. Marlowe asks us to view the entire action before judging Faustus, and so presents him that unequivocal moral judgment is impossible.

The strange course begins directly Faustus has made his choice. In the upsurge of his arrogance he feels confident and secure. He ridicules such notions as "hell" and "damnation" and "these vain trifles of men's souls." He is elated with the success of his first conjuring (Scene 3), reproves the fainthearted Mephistophilis, and sends him to strike the twenty-four-year bargain with Lucifer. In a similar mood, after signing the contract in blood, he calls hell a "fable" and the threat of eternal torment an "old wives' tale." "Ay," says Mephistophilis, "think so, till experience change thy mind." It is Faustus' redeeming quality that experience *could* change his mind and that he is sensitive to every stage of the process. By the time of his second conjuring (Scene 5), even before the signing, he confesses doubts. "Something soundeth in mine ears," he says—a voice that calls upon him to abjure his magic and turn to God again. "Why waverest thou?" he asks himself. "Be resolute." As he comes ever closer to the edge of the known and the tried, a glimpse into the abyss brings a moment of intense self-realization:

> Ay, and Faustus will turn to God again.
> To God? He loves thee not;
> The God thou servest is thine own appetite.

In the dialogue with the Good and Evil Angels, immediately following, the tone with which he speaks of "Contrition, prayer, repentance —what of them?" is hesitant and nostalgic. "Sweet Faustus—" pleads the Good Angel, and Faustus seems for a moment to yield, only to be drawn back to his arrogant ways by the Evil Angel's reminder of

[4] Indeed, as Herbert Weisinger suggests (*Tragedy and the Paradox of the Fortunate Fall,* E. Lansing, Michigan State College Press, 1953, p. 10), the doctrine of the *felix culpa* springs from the same archetypal experience. Just as the primitive king or hero—and later, the Savior—taking upon himself the sins of the people, died sacrificially, was reborn and brought new life, so the tragic hero in his pride "sins," dies, and brings us "new life." Weisinger sees the secularization of the paradox of the fortunate fall as "the substance out of which tragedy, and particularly Shakespearean tragedy, is made."

honor and of wealth that now lie within his power. "Of wealth!" cries
Faustus,

> Why, the signiory of Emden shall be mine.
> When Mephistophilis shall stand by me
> What God can hurt me? Faustus, thou art safe:
> Cast no more doubts.

But the doubts will not vanish, and Faustus lives out his twenty-
four-year gamble as the first modern tragic man, part believer, part
unbeliever, vacillating between independence and dependence upon
God, now arrogant and confident, now anxious and worried, justified
yet horribly unjustified. He is forced constantly to renew his choice
between two awesome alternatives, and in the opposite phases of the
rhythm he sees greater and more glorious heights, and depths of
greater terror. Soon the gentle voice that "sounded" in his ears, bidding
him abjure his magic and return to God, becomes the fearful thundering echoes: "Faustus, thou art damned!" What he is learning is the
truth of his own nature—a truth which it was his peculiar Renaissance
compulsion to forget or deny: that he is creature as well as creator; a
man and not a god; a dependent, responsible part of a greater whole.
He learns that his soul is not a mere trifle of his own, to use as a
commodity, and that "contrition, prayer, repentance," hell and damnation, are not (as the Evil Angel told him)

> . . . illusions, fruits of lunacy,
> That make men foolish that do trust them most.

Like Koestler's Rubashov (in *Darkness at Noon*) he had "forgotten
the infinite" and the humbling terror with which it invests all the
undertakings of man.

Pressing on in spite of the echoes and the doubts, he reaches levels
of perception never gained by the less venturous. Like Job, he was not
content with having "heard by the hearing of the ear"; he must see
with his own eyes. He has frivolous moments (some of them surely not
of Marlowe's conceiving), when he boxes the Pope's ears and gets
grapes in January. But the random wishes of his early days of conjuring take a more salutary direction. He does not want so much
what power will bring—he never takes the Signiory of Emden, never
walls Germany with brass, never clothes the schoolboys in silk. He
wants what all men, good and bad, have wanted; to conquer time,
space, and ignorance. Above all he wants knowledge: what is hell?
where is it? who made the world—"the plants, the herbs, the trees that
grow upon the earth"? He cruises hither and yon in the world and
above it, exploring all climes and the secrets of the heavens. He
delves into the past, makes "blind Homer sing," Amphion play the

harp, and Helen appear for a dazzling moment. What Marlowe dramatizes is not only the terror of the black art as the old story told about it
and as we see it reflected (in the play) in the eyes of the lesser characters, The Old Man, Wagner, and The Scholars, but the wonder of
it—the wonder of the man who dared use it and the wonder of the
mysteries it unfolds.[5]

But within the wonder is the terror of its fascination and compulsion, beckoning man into the peculiar dilemma of modern times. On
the one hand is human limitation and finiteness, the necessary
postulate and the first step in the Christian experience. On the other,
with the old catechism wearing thin, it is the compulsion of modern
man to deny his limitations, press ever further into the mysteries of a
universe which appears steadily to yield more and more of its secrets
to his inquiring mind. To rest content with his limitations seems to
deny his own God-given powers; and yet to challenge the mystery is
somehow evil and portends not only present suffering but, such are the
echoes that thunder in his ears, the horrors of eternity.

> Why wert thou not a creature wanting soul?
> Or why is this immortal that thou hast?

asks Faustus in his last despairing moments. To the medieval theology
which held that man *is* because he believes, the Renaissance replied
that man is because he thinks and acts and discovers. Neither one, as
Marlowe presents Faustus' dilemma, is wholly right or wholly wrong.
The world of certainties is no longer intact, and we are only a step
from the riddles and the eternal questioning that harassed the Karamazovs. In the world of tragedy, the hero can only take the road of
experiment. He must follow his bent, take action, and live it through.
By contrast, in Goethe's version of the story, Faust has divine sanction.
"The Prologue in Heaven" dramatizes a quite different universe, as
amidst its harmonies God specifically commends Faust's inquiring
mind and authorizes the pact with the Devil. The Goethean Faust
knows melancholy and frustration. He gets himself (and Gretchen)

[5] Paul H. Kocher, in his introduction to *Doctor Faustus* (Crofts Classics ed., New
York, Appleton-Century-Crofts, 1950, p. viii), sees this, on whatever authority, as
related directly to Marlowe's personal experiences: ". . . his imagination leaped to
the wonder and terror of the deeds of magic, and the religious conflict drew powerfully on feelings which he was undergoing in his own life. It was for him the
perfect theme." It is worth noting, now that we have reached in our study the era
of modern drama when biographical information accumulates, that such suggestions—they can seldom be more than that—about the "involvement" of the artist
in his fictions increase. Berdyaev, for instance, makes them repeatedly about
Dostoevski: "The destiny of his characters is his own, their doubts and dualities
are his, their iniquities are the sins hidden in his own soul." (*Dostoievsky*, p. 32).
—My quotations from *Doctor Faustus* are from the Crofts Classics edition throughout.

into a sad scrape. But he never experiences the terror of the Elizabethan hero's dilemma or takes so bold a risk or suffers his despair. He
adjusts himself nicely to Gretchen's death, and in the end his actions
are brought into harmony with good nineteenth-century humanitarian-
ism.

The end of Marlowe's play shows, of course, that (like the tragic
Karamazovs) Faustus could not live out his idea. But between the
disillusioned scholar of the first scene and the agonizing, ecstatic
figure of the final scene there is a notable difference. He enters, not
alone this time, but with the Scholars; and for the first time in the
play he has normal, compassionate discourse with his fellows. His role
of demigod over, he is human once more, a friend and befriended.
"Ah, gentlemen, hear me with patience," says he who has but recently lorded it over all creation. His friends now seem more "sweet"
(as he thrice addresses them) than any princely delicate or Signiory of
Emden. Although the thrill of his exploits still lingers— "And what
wonders I have done all Germany can witness, yea all the world . . ."
—he is humble and repentant. He longs to be able to weep and pray
but imagines in his despair that devils draw in his tears and hold his
hands as he would lift them up. He confesses to the Scholars the
miserable source of his cunning. Knowing his doom is near, he refuses
their intercession and bids them "Talk not of me, but save yourselves
and depart." They retire, like Oedipus' children at Colonus, for the
hero to meet his fate alone. "Gentlemen, farewell," he says as they
go. "If I live till morning I'll visit you; if not, Faustus is gone to hell."

If to the orthodox it is more a sinner's fate than a hero's, there is
something of the classic apotheosis in Faustus' final moments. He
transcends the man he was. He goes out no craven sinner but
violently, speaking the rage and despair of all mankind who would
undo the past and stop the clock against the inevitable reckoning.
The grandeur of conception of his earlier worldly imaginings gains a
kind of sublimity.

> Stand still, you ever-moving spheres of heaven,
> That time may cease and midnight never come.

Like Job in the agony of his suffering, he has visions never vouchsafed
in his days of prosperity. The nearer to Hell, the closer he is to
Heaven:

> O I'll leap up to my God! Who pulls me down?
> See, see, where Christ's blood streams in the firmament!—
> One drop would save my soul—half a drop! ah, my Christ!

He asks no questions now; he sees with his own eyes: first the Christ of
mercy, then the God of wrath as He "Stretcheth out his arm and bends

his ireful brows." He longs to be hidden under hills, thence to be borne aloft to heaven in the volcano's breath; he would be dissolved into a cloud and thus ascend; he would be turned into a beast with no immortal soul: "All beasts are happy. . . ." It is eternity that appals him, the consequence of his living, immortal soul. He curses the parents who engendered him, he curses Lucifer, and (most justly) himself. He does not hide his eyes. "My God, my God, look not so fierce on me!"

> Adders and serpents, let me breathe awhile!
> Ugly hell, gape not—come not, Lucifer—
> I'll burn my books—ah, Mephistophilis!

The Devils lead him off, amidst thunder. If he is more sinning than sinned against, he yet has shown great capacities for good as well as evil, and we cannot feel that perfect justice has been done. Theologically, of course, Faustus in his extremity was mistaken: it is never too late to ask and receive God's mercy and pardon. Or, does Marlowe present him as still unpurged of his pride ("And what wonders I have done all Germany can witness, yea all the world. . . ."), a sinner not wholly repentant? He does not completely abase himself in self-loathing (as a good Christian would) nor accept without demur a fate which he knows, according to the contract, is just. Rather, he resists his fate, imagines impossible evasions, clings to every precious second of remaining life. Perhaps Marlowe believed that Faustus was doomed no matter how humble his repentance; or he may have conceived him as so hardened in his rationalism as to believe faith a mere function of reason. But the final scene gives a sense, not so much of the justice and goodness of the universe as of the transcendent human individual, caught in the consequences of a dilemma which, granted the conditions of his times, it was impossible for any imaginative man wholly to avoid.

The Nature of Faustus' Fall

by Douglas Cole

There is no denying the fact that in *Doctor Faustus,* Christopher Marlowe, whatever his personal views of Christianity may have been, has fashioned a play that is thoroughly Christian in conception and import. Christianity was of course explicit in Marlowe's source, the English Faust-Book. But in adapting that meandering collection of anecdotes about the famous German magician, Marlowe gave it a new, concentrated, intellectual shape by reorganizing his material along the more sophisticated lines of philosophical and theological concepts of evil. As a result, his play carries much more meaning than simply, "Don't sell your soul to the devil." The moral of the English Faust-Book is little more than that.

The depiction of Faustus' motivation for adhering to magic and the service of the devil is scant and sketchy in the Faust-Book. We learn that Faustus dabbled in magic even before becoming a Doctor of Divinity, "being of a naughty minde & otherwise addicted."[1] Though "excellent perfect in the holy scriptures," he "waxed a worldly man," devoting himself to magic, astrology, mathematics and medicine (i, 136). In the interests of his worldly pleasure he "thought to flie ouer the whole world, and to know the secrets of heauen and earth" (ii, 137). And thus he began to conjure.

What Marlowe has made of this vague hint of worldly speculation can best be understood against the background of the Christian theology of sin current in his time. That theology had been given its classic and enduring formulation by St. Augustine, whose work was drawn upon by Catholic and Protestant theologians alike. The Lady Margaret Professor of Theology at Cambridge in Marlowe's university

[1] *The Historie of the damnable life, and deserued death of Doctor Iohn Faustus* (London, 1592), eds. Philip Mason Palmer and Robert Pattison More in *The Sources of the Faust Tradition from Simon Magus to Lessing* (New York, 1936), ch. i, p. 135. Subsequent references to this edition will appear in my text.

years, Peter Baro, had the highest esteem for Augustine, calling him "the prince of theologians";[2] and it is practically certain that Marlowe, as a student of theology, had firsthand acquaintance with his work.[3] In the view of Augustine, man, like the angels before him, was created with the power to move upward to God, in fulfillment of the purpose for which he was made, or downward to degradation and misery. "All sins," he writes in the *De libero arbitrio*, "consist in turning away from godly things which are truly lasting, and in turning towards things which are changeable and insecure."[4] "The will sins," he continues, "if it turns away from the unchangeable good which is common to all, and turns towards a private good, whether outside or below it. . . . Thus a man who becomes proud, curious, and self-indulgent, is caught up in another life, which compared to the higher life is death."[5] Thus the perverted will is the cause of all evil, and the root of that perversion lies in the impulses of pride and egoism. If the soul should go out of its way "to produce a false imitation of God, and to will to take pleasure in its own power, then the greater it wishes to become, the less it becomes in fact. And that is *pride, the beginning of all sin; and the beginning of the pride of man is to fall off from God.*"[6]

Now it is obvious that a theological formulation such as this can apply to practically any human sin whatsoever, given enough meditation and analysis. Certainly the Elizabethan audience need not have had recourse to such ideas in order to evaluate Faustus' action in selling his soul to the devil. But the interesting thing is that when one looks at the way in which Marlowe has chosen to present *his* Doctor Faustus, as contrasted with the Faust-Book presentation, it is clear that the theological ideas and concepts involved in the Augustinian definition of moral evil are transposed *directly* into dramatic language and action.

[2] *In Jonam Prophetam Prælectiones 39* (London, 1579), Tt2ᵛ.

[3] The Parker collection in the Corpus Christi College Library in Marlowe's time included an eight-volume printed edition of Augustine's works, the largest edition of any one theologian in the entire printed book collection. MS. 575, p. 5.

[4] *The Problem of Free Choice*, trans. Dom Mark Pontifex (Westminster, Maryland, 1955), I.16.35, p. 72.

[5] *Ibid.*, II.19.53, p. 135.

[6] *Ibid.*, III.25.76, pp. 218–219. This notion, of course, which derives from Ecclesiasticus X.14–15, was to become a theological commonplace, familiar not only to students of theology, but to all who were instructed in the barest rudiments of the Christian religion. One of the homilies officially appointed by Elizabeth to be read on Sundays throughout her realm began "Of our going frō God, the wise man saith, that pride was the first beginning: for by it mans hearte was turned from God his maker. For pride (saith he) is the fountaine of all sinne: he that hath it, shal be ful of cursings, and at the ende it shal ouerthrow him." *Certaine Sermons appointed by the Queenes Maiestie, to be declared and read, by all Parsons, Vicars and Curates, every Sunday and Holy day in their Churches: and by her graces aduice perused and ouerseene, for the better understanding of the simple people* (London, 1582), E2.

One does not have to look behind the words and actions to discover Faustus' pride, the willfulness of his falling from God, or his egoistic ambition to become his own god; they are outwardly and directly manifest in everything he says and does.

The opening Chorus describes the man, his intellectual excellence, and his fatal choice:

> . . . swolne with cunning, of a selfe conceit,
> His waxen wings did mount aboue his reach,
> And melting, heauens conspir'd his ouer-throw:
> For falling to a diuellishex ercise, [*sic*]
> And glutted now with learnings golden gifts,
> He surfets vpon cursed Necromancie:
> Nothing so sweet as Magicke is to him;
> Which he preferres before his chiefest blisse. . . .
>
> (20–27)

The picture and the issue is clear enough; the allusion to Icarus, a familiar Elizabethan symbol of self-destructive aspiration, [7] is emblematic of Faustus' career, while the alternative between "cursed Necromancie" and "his chiefest bliss" is set forth as the object of Faustus' deliberate choice.

Marlowe devotes his first scene to a careful presentation of Faustus' decision to take up magic. One by one Faustus examines the branches of higher learning as they were organized in the universities of his day: philosophy, medicine, law, and theology. One by one the fields of secular learning are rejected because their ends do not satisfy his demand—but notice what the demand is. He does not pursue knowledge for the sake of truth, but for power, superhuman power, the power over life and death. His fundamental grievance is "Yet art thou still but *Faustus,* and a man" (50). Dissatisfied with his creature status, rebelling against the limitations which define the mode of human existence, he would like to make men live eternally, or to raise the

---

[7] Icarus was a familiar figure in emblem books of the sixteenth century, appearing under the text "In astrologos" in Alciati and Whitney, and under "Faire tout par moyen" in Corrozet. See Henry Green, *Shakespeare and the Emblem Writers* (London, 1870), pp. 288–290. The prologue to Thomas Preston's *Cambises* had drawn a simile between Icarus and the king to illustrate Cambises' self-will:

> "Then cleauing more vnto his wil such vice did immitate:
> As one of *Icarus* his kind, forewarning then did hate.
> Thinking that none could him dismay, ne none his fact could see,
> Yet at the last a fall he tooke, like *Icarus* to be."

Cambises king of Percia (TFT, 1910), A2. In the Induction to *The First parte of the Mirour for Magistrates* (1574) Icarus is used as an example of destructive ambition: *Parts Added to The Mirror for Magistrates by John Higgins & Thomas Blenerhasset,* ed. Lily B. Campbell (Cambridge, 1946), p. 42.

dead—secularized parodies of the activities of the Christian God.
Divine learning is cast aside as well: because, as Helen Gardner's sensitive interpretation suggests, "it is grounded in the recognition of man's
mortality and his fallibility."[8]

> *Ieromes* Bible *Faustus*, view it well:
> *Stipendium peccati, mors est: ha, stipendium, &c.*
> The reward of sin is death? that's hard:
> *Si peccasse, negamus, fallimur, & nulla est in nobis veritas:*
> If we say that we haue no sinne
> We deceiue our selues, and there is no truth in vs.
> Why then belike we must sinne,
> And so consequently die,
> I, we must die, an euerlasting death.
> What doctrine call you this? *Che sera, sera:*
> What will be, shall be; *Diuinitie* adeiw.
>
>   (65–75)

Faustus leaves Divinity to God, and dedicates himself to the devil.
Scorning the fatality of "What will be, shall be," he performs his own
act of will, and it is one of the developing ironies of the play that what
he wills to be shall be.

The facile syllogism by which Faustus rejects the Scriptures and
Divinity is in itself a deeply ironic comment on the Doctor's character
and career. Its sophistry is really only an excuse for Faustus to turn to
his true aspiration:

> O what a world of profite and delight,
> Of power, of honour, and omnipotence,
> Is promised to the Studious Artizan?
>
>   (80–82)

But beyond its rationalizing function, Faustus' syllogism betrays not
only a deep-seated willingness to pervert the Scriptures, but also the
foreshadowing of an attitude of mind that will gradually lead him to
the sin of despair. It is, in sum, the real point of his fall from God.

Faustus arrives at his fatalistic conclusion by joining together two
premises which themselves are glaring half-truths, for each of the
propositions he cites from the Bible is drawn from contexts and passages which unite the helplessness of the sinner with the redeeming
grace of God. The first, from Romans vi.23, concludes a chapter which
stresses how the Christian has been freed from the bondage of sin by
Christ's redemption; in its complete form it reads, "For the wages of
sinne is death: but the gifte of God *is* eternal life through Jesus Christ

---

[8] "Milton's 'Satan' and the Theme of Damnation," p. 49.

our Lord" [9] The second, from 1 John i.8, is also part of an antithetical construction; the clause Faustus cites is followed by "If we acknowledge our sinnes, he is faithful and iust, to forgiue vs our sinnes, & to clense vs from all vnrighteousness." [10] Faustus' error of stopping halfway in this text could not easily have gone unnoticed by the Elizabethan audience. The second of the official Elizabethan sermons and homilies opened with a series of scriptural references to the sinful condition of man, among them the very one Faustus uses: "So doth blessed Saint Iohn the Euangelist, in the name of himselfe, and of al other holy men (be they neuer so iust) make this open confession: If we say we haue no sinne, we deceyue ourselues, and the truth is not in vs: If we knowledge our sinnes, God is faythfull and iust to forgiue our sinnes, and to cleanse vs from all vnrighteousnesse." [11]

The sermon goes on to exhort that the state of mortal imperfection be acknowledged, but also that the mercy of God and Christ's saving merits be relied upon to raise man from his misery. Faustus, at this point in his career, sees only the imperfection, not the opportunity of redemption—he scornfully casts away the whole doctrine; at a later point, consciousness of his sinfulness will be painfully present, but his self-imposed blindness will continue to shut out the light of proffered salvation.

Faustus is blinded here by precisely the same flash of "logic" which the devil in Thomas Becon's *Dialogue Between the Christian Knight and Satan* (1564) employs (also in a syllogism) to tempt the knight to despair, and which in Spenser's *Faerie Queene* Despair uses to tempt Red Cross to spiritual death.[12] Faustus' desperation will be a torment to him in the future; now it spurs him to indulge in his own dreams of power. His attitude and decision are exact replicas of the thoughts of the reprobate described by Wolfgang Musculus, whose theological works were read and esteemed in the schools of Reformation England: "Why shoulde I trouble and trauell my selfe in vaine? and doe those things whiche doe like my mind, seeyng that I do know I am determined to destruction?" [13]

There is one final irony in Faustus' rejection of Divinity by a trick

[9] The translation is that of the Geneva Bible (1560).

[10] *Ibid.*

[11] *Certaine Sermons*, A7ᵛ.

[12] Kocher has noted the similarity to Becon's work: *Christopher Marlowe*, pp. 106–107; Virgil K. Whitaker has remarked on the resemblance to Spenser's: *Shakespeare's Use of Learning: An Inquiry into the Growth of his Mind and Art* (San Marino, Calif., 1953), p. 242.

[13] *Common Places of Christian Religion*, trans. John Man (London, 1578), p. 1093 (zzz3). The Parker collection in the Corpus Christi Library included two editions of the *Common Places* of Musculus. MS. 575, pp. 15–16.

of reason, and it lies in the distinction drawn by theologians between Divinity and the other disciplines. Calvin went so far as to posit two different understandings in man, one of terrestrial things, and another of celestial ones.[14] The latter concerned the knowledge of God, his Divine Will, and man's conformity to it; but without the aid of God's grace, man's reason when directed toward these objects was totally blind and stupid. [15] Peter Baro wrote that the dignity of theology rested in the fact that only in this discipline was the Spirit of God at work as a teacher, rather than reason alone; but this Spirit would only be efficacious when the student's attitude was open and reverent.[16] Faustus' syllogism, then, is as arrogant as it is facile, and in the last analysis a destructive manipulation of thought and reason. The horror with which the sophisticated Christian looked upon such an act has been given eloquent form by John Donne, in a sermon excerpt that is itself a yardstick for the kinds of evil that Marlowe has exhibited in both this play and others: "Whilst we sin strongly, by oppressing others, that are weaker, or craftily by circumventing others that are simple, This is but *Leoninum,* and *Vulpinum,* that tincture of the Lyon, and of the Fox, that brutal nature that is in us. But when we come to sin, upon reason, and upon discourse, upon Meditation, and upon plot, This is *Humanum,* to become the Man of Sin, to surrender that, which is the Form, and Essence of man, Reason, and understanding, to the service of sin. When we come to sin wisely and learnedly, to sin logically, by a *Quia,* and an *Ergo,* that, Because God does thus, we may do as we do, we shall come to sin through all the Arts, and all our knowledge." [17]

Yet Donne's description of the "Man of Sin" does not completely cover the gravity of Faustus' decision and desire as Marlowe has presented it in this initial monologue. For Doctor Faustus aspires to be more than man. As he lingers lovingly over his necromantic books and occult characters, he foresees personal power over all the world:

> All things that moue betweene the quiet Poles
> Shall be at my command. . . .
>
> .   .   .   .
>
> A sound Magitian is a Demi-god,
> Here tire my braines to get a Deity.

> (83–89)

---

[14] John Calvin, *Institutes of the Christian Religion,* II.ii.13, trans. John Allen, 7th American ed. (Philadelphia, [1936]), I, 294.

[15] *Ibid.,* II.ii.19; II, 299–300.

[16] *In Jonam Prophetam,* pp. 3, 5–6 (A2, A3–A3ᵛ).

[17] *Sermons,* I, 225.

The Augustinian formulation of sin is here filled out, and the bonds that will link Faustus with Lucifer are forged by Faustus himself. [18] He repudiates his humanity, rebelling against the ultimate reality; in his aspiration to be as God he chooses the not-God. This is the essential irony of sin, and the central irony of the play. In the Christian view of the world, it is inevitable that choice of the not-God will lead not only to disappointment but also to the deepest suffering.

[18] Donne's words are again to the point: ". . . for the greatest sin that ever was, and that upon which even the blood of Christ Jesus hath not wrought, the sin of Angels, was that, *Similis ero Altissimo*, to be like God." *Sermons*, IV, 330.

Religious Values in *Doctor Faustus*

by *Leo Kirschbaum*

Marlowe's Faustus has so often been described by modern critics as a superman, reaching out for infinite knowledge and ineffable beauty, as an individual whom we ought proudly to esteem as representative of aspiring humanity, that one almost hesitates to disagree with this well-nigh universal opinion. Yet, surprisingly, it is unsupported by the play itself. One surmises that such a view of Faustus is a fiction derived ultimately from reactions against medievalism, against Christianity, and against past assertions of man's fundamental weakness and limits. The nineteenth and early twentieth centuries, with their faith in science and progress, and with their concept of man's yet unrealized potentialities, tended to reject any view, be it religion or philosophy, which denied this faith and this concept. Thus it has come about that Marlowe's protagonist has been chosen as a symbol of the "new" man. Critics, frankly, have been unable to see the drama in its own terms, have persisted in seeing it in the light of our own *Zeitgeist*.

Only recently has the literary tide begun to turn. Indulgent empathy for Marlowe's magician is slowly being supplanted by a more objective appraisal. Rid of present-day preconceptions, whether they be borrowed from the critics or supplied by ourselves, we are beginning to perceive that the late sixteenth century drama *Doctor Faustus* is wholly conventional in its Christian values and is in no sense iconoclastic. St. Thomas Aquinas would have approved of its innate doctrine. And Richard Hooker could have used it as an exemplum to teach the correct Christian path to God. Nor would Luther, Calvin, or Knox—the founders of European Protestantism—have found anything inflammatory in it. Marlowe's play is in no way destructive of the basic tenets of Christianity. On the contrary, it enforces and illuminates those very tenets.

There is no more obvious Christian document in all Elizabethan drama than the play under discussion. Let the reader or spectator forget about the paganism of the Renaissance or the sectism of the Refor-

"*Religious Values in* Doctor Faustus." *From* The Plays of Christopher Marlowe, ed. Leo Kirschbaum (*Cleveland and New York: The World Publishing Company, 1962*), *pp. 101–13. Copyright © 1962 by the World Publishing Company. Reprinted by permission of the publisher.*

mation. Let us see the play in the terms of the basic Christian values
it preaches, for it is, we must recognize, a morality play. Let us examine
the play Marlowe wrote—which is not the play most critics think he
wrote, not the play some critics want him to have written.

In the theater watching *Doctor Faustus,* or in the study reading it,
we must, for the nonce, either accept its values or choose some other
drama more congenial to our beliefs and tastes. We must accept, for the
occasion, that man's most precious possession is his immortal soul and
that what he does on earth will determine whether he goes to Heaven
or Hell, whether after his worldy life he will enjoy perpetual bliss with
God or perpetual pain with the Devil. (We need not get mired here in
debate about the Calvinistic doctrine of the elect: those who are chosen
reveal their future sanctity by their earthly conduct.) The premises of
basic Christianity are inherent in every line of *Doctor Faustus.* The
doctrine of damnation pervades it.

In the play the Devil and Hell are omnipresent, potent, dangerous,
and terrifying realities. But the protagonist makes a bargain with
Evil, and for the sake of earthly learning, earthly power, earthly
satisfaction goes down to horrible and everlasting perdition. As we shall
observe, it is actually a poor bargain, for the gains of knowledge and
power are largely offset by egocentric self-satisfaction. Marlowe portrays
his "hero" as a wretched creature who for lower values gives up higher
ones. Thus, the drama is a morality play in which Heaven combats
with Hell for the soul of a Renaissance Everyman and, due to the
latter's psychological and moral weaknesses, loses.

Faustus' apostrophe to Helen of Troy in the last act has again and
again been presented as a pagan paean to beauty, Marlowe's own sensuous declaration of sensual delight, a declaration of Renaissance man's
newfound freedom:

> Was this the face that launch'd a thousand ships *ff.*
>
> (5.1.92–111).

Here, say the critics, Marlowe celebrates the program of modern man,
who has at last fully escaped the contempt of the world and the flesh
which the Middle Ages taught. But before we reread this passage, let us
see it in the context of the play. I believe that we will find that the passage signals the protagonist's final defeat by the powers of darkness.

I think I should stress here that the viable eschatology of the play is
so rigid that ambivalence in interpretation is ruled out. If the modern
mind, for example, sees Marlowe's main character as the noble victim
of a tyrannical Deity, it is simply being blind. On the contrary, God is
exceedingly good in his gifts to the "hero," until the latter becomes the
victim of his own insatiable desires—and even then God is willing to
forgive if the magician repents. But Faustus willfully refuses all aid—

and so goes down to damnation. No, there is no ambiguity on the main issues in the play. But there is much irony, which Marlowe skillfully employs.

The dramatist establishes the viable values of his drama by various means: by the Choruses; by Faustus' own recognition; by the Good Angel; by Mephostophilis, interestingly enough; by the Old Man—and, of course, by the action itself. I am not thinking merely of the macabre ending. As an example of the pervasive Christian viewpoint, there is, for example, the cumulative coarsening of the magician's character and his indulgence in cheap, sadistic fun: this is due to *habitude,* constant indulgence in sin.

The Prologue, or First Chorus, sets Faustus, his character and his doom, before us in clear, emphatic terms:

> So much he profits in divinity
> That shortly he was grac'd with doctor's name,
> Excelling all, and sweetly can dispute
> In th' heavenly matters of theology—
> Till swoll'n with cunning, of a self-conceit,
> His waxen wings did mount above his reach
> And melting, Heavens conspir'd his over-throw!
> For falling to a devilish exercise
> And glutted now with learning's golden gifts
> He surfeits upon cursed necromancy:
> Nothing so sweet as magic is to him
> Which he prefers before his chiefest bliss. . . .
> And this the man that in his study sits.

We must trust Marlowe's *ex cathedra* description of his protagonist— a man who, swollen with pride in his attainments, comes to a deserved end because he has preferred forbidden pursuits to "his chiefest bliss." (Certainly Marlowe guides us deftly by the analogy with Icarus—who, of course, equates with Lucifer.) The Faustus whom Marlowe gives us in the ensuing action is both more complex and less radiant than the utterances of most critics would lead us to expect.

At the very beginning of Faustus' temptation, the Good Angel—the voice of God, the expounder of things as they are, the opponent of the Bad Angel, who is the emissary of Satan—declares:

> O, Faustus, lay that damned book aside
> And gaze not on it lest it tempt thy soul
> And heap God's heavy wrath upon thy head!
> Read, read the Scriptures—that is blasphemy!

But Faustus hearkens to the Bad Angel. And note what he expects as a reward for practicing the forbidden black magic. Before the Good Angel enters, he gloats:

> O, what a world of profit and delight,
> Of power, of honor, and omnipotence
> Is promis'd to the studious artisan!

He not only will get knowledge and power: his mind also dwells long-ingly on satisfaction of material appetite. The spirits will bring him "gold," "orient pearl," "pleasant fruits," "princely delicates," and "silk."

Faustus has intellectual pride to an odious degree, but he is also avid for more vainglory:

> And I, that have with subtle syllogisms
> Gravell'd the pastors of the German church
> And made the flow'ring pride of Wittenberg
> (Swarm) to my problems, as th' infernal spirits
> On sweet Musaeus when he came to Hell,
> Will be as cunning as Agrippa was,
> Whose shadows made all Europe honor him.

Faustus is wholly egocentric. To himself, be is either the greatest of men, or the greatest of abject sinners. He underrates his opponents, and relishes his inflated sense of his own abilities. Thus, after Mephostoph-ilis has left the stage at the behest of the magician that he reappear in the more pleasant guise of a Franciscan (Marlowe is indeed subtle: Faustus will not and cannot accept things as they are: the truth must be side-stepped some way, the bitter pill must be coated with sugar), Faustus wallows in a delusion of self-importance:

> How pliant is this Mephostophilis,
> Full of obedience and humility,
> Such is the force of magic and my spells!

But Mephostophilis quickly disillusions him:

> *Faust.* Did not my conjuring raise thee? Speak.
> *Meph.* That was the cause, but yet *per accidens:*
> For when we hear one rack the name of God,
> Abjure the Scriptures and his Savior Christ,
> We fly in hope to get his glorious soul.
> Nor will we come unless he use such means
> Whereby he is in danger to be damn'd.
> Therefore the shortest cut for conjuring
> Is stoutly to abjure all godliness
> And pray devoutly to the Prince of Hell.

Faustus agrees to worship Belzebub:

> This word *damnation* terrifies not me
> For I confound hell in Elysium:
> My ghost be with the old philosophers!
> But, leaving these vain trifles of men's souls,
> Tell me, what is that Lucifer thy lord?

But note how Marlowe immediately shows up the vanity and fool-hardiness of this last speech. In order to set forth that damnation and soul are not mere trifles, the playwright has the enemy of man strip Faustus of those very delusions which the enemy of man wants Faustus to possess in order that the enemy of man may destroy Faustus. The enemy of the truth supports the truth so that the audience will be absolutely clear as to what the truth is. And mark that Mephostophilis foreshadows Faustus' fall in Lucifer's, and that insolence and pride are the instigators in both cases:

> *Faust.* Was not that Lucifer an angel once? *ff.*
>
>   (1.3.61–79).

But the foolhardy Faustus, having been warned by the Devil himself, reprimands the latter for cowardliness! He boasts:

> What, is great Mephostophilis so passionate
> For being deprived of the joys of Heaven?
> Learn thou of Faustus manly fortitude
> And scorn those joys thou never shalt possess.

How can any one read the scene and call the self-deluded, foolishly boastful Faustus a superman?

Note carefully what Faustus wants in return for selling his soul to the Devil:

> Say, he surrenders up to him his soul
> So he will spare him four and twenty years,
> Letting him live in all voluptuousness,
> Having thee ever to attend on me,
> To give me whatsoever I shall ask,
> To tell me whatsoever I demand,
> To slay mine enemies and to aid my friends
> And always be obedient to my will.

Utter satisfaction of the will and utter satisfaction of the senses are what Faustus desires. And how he prates—who a little later will be quaking!

> Had I as many souls as there be stars,
> I'd give them all for Mephostophilis!

The next time we see Faustus, midnight of the same day, his emotional and intellectual instability is fully revealed. He veers between God and the Devil. At first he is conscience-stricken. All his cocky effrontery is gone. But in a moment he is once more the user of egocentric hyperbole:

> Now, Faustus, must thou needs be damn'd, canst thou not be sav'd *ff*.
>
> (2.1.1–12).

A weakling, he must cover his fears with megalomaniacal fantasy. Two points should be made. We must understand that Faustus' conclusion as to the impossibility of God's mercy is the mark of a diseased ego—a lack of humility. And also, we must particularly remark Faustus' self-recognition of his driving passion: "The god thou serv'st is thine own appetite."

The struggle between Faustus' uncontrolled appetite and the powers of Heaven continues:

> *Enter the two Angels.*
> *Bad Ang.* Go forward, Faustus, in that famous art.
> *Good Ang.* Sweet Faustus, leave that execrable art. *ff*.
>
> (2.1.13–25).

He thus deludes himself: "What power can hurt me?" But again Faustus is warned by the emissary of Hell what awaits him if he sells his soul to the Devil:

> *Faust.* Stay, Mephostophilis, and tell me
> What good my soul will do thy lord?
> *Meph.* Enlarge his kingdom.
> *Faust.* Is that the reason why he tempts us thus?
> *Meph. Solamen miseris socios habuisse doloris.*
> *Faust.* Why, have you any pain that torture other?
> *Meph.* As great as have the human souls of men.

And that Faustus has free will, free choice, ability to affirm or deny God if he so wishes; that he cannot (as he does later) blame anyone but himself for his act and its consequences, Faustus himself makes clear when, after his blood has congealed so that he cannot sign the document and give his soul to Hell, he says:

> Why streams it not that I may write afresh:
> "Faustus gives to thee his soul?" O there it stay'd. . . .
> Why shouldst thou not? Is not thy soul thine own?
> Then write again: "Faustus gives to thee his soul."

Marlowe's powers of compressed dramatic irony can be tremendous. As soon as Faustus has signed, he says *"Consummatum est,"* the last words of Christ on earth according to St. John. What an insight into the twisted mind of the magician! And what blasphemy! Jesus died that Faustus' soul might live; Faustus flings away this priceless gift for a mess of earthly pottage! But the words are also true in a more literal sense: the good life, the possibility of reaching Heaven, are indeed being finished for Faustus.

When, immediately afterward, God's warning *"Homo fuge!"* appears on Faustus' arm, he—characteristically—affirms the God whom he has just denied and gets into a turmoil of conflicting impulses:

> *Homo fuge!* Whither should I fly?
> If unto Heav'n, He'll throw me down to Hell.
> —My senses are deceiv'd, here's nothing writ.
> —O yes, I see it plain! Even here is writ
> *Homo fuge!* Yet shall not Faustus fly!

Hence, Faustus consciously and deliberately sets his will against God's. But as he is in this state, Mephostophilis, knowing his victim, says in an aside, "I'll fetch him somewhat to delight his mind." And then to the voluptuary *"Enter Devils, giving crowns and rich apparel to Faustus. They dance and then depart."*

Thus, Mephostophilis deliberately offers Faustus sensual satisfaction in order to distract his mind from spiritual concern—which might, of course, lead to repentance. This pattern is a basic one in the play, and an understanding of it will eventually enable us to interpret truly the Helen of Troy apostrophe. Whenever there is danger, from the Devil's viewpoint, that Faustus will turn to God's mercy, the powers of Hell will deaden their victim's conscience by providing him with some great satisfaction of the senses. But sometimes Faustus will ask for the opiate himself.

In the same scene, Faustus receives a true description of his condition, but cheaply flaunts his disbelief—as though one should deny gravity! Once more it is Mephostophilis who forcefully establishes the values:

Faust. I think Hell's a fable.
Meph. Ay, think so still—till experience change thy mind! *ff.* (2.1.124–35).

And here, again, Marlowe shows the constitution of Faustus' mind. As soon as Mephostophilis has stated that Hell with its tortures and damnation do exist, Faustus asks for his customary anodyne for uncomfortable conscience:

Faust. Nay, and this be Hell, I'll willingly be damn'd—What, sleeping, eating, walking, and disputing? But leaving this, let me have a wife, the fairest maid in Germany, for I am wanton and lascivious and cannot live without a wife. *ff.* (2.1.135–50).

See again Marlowe's compressed irony—Faustus shall have his appetite satisfied by women as beautiful "As was bright Lucifer before his fall."

In the next scene (2.2), the Devil's agent and Faustus are again together. Faustus is going through another of his struggles between repentance and nonrepentance. He blames Mephostophilis for his misery, but the latter points out that the magician made his choice of his own free will: " 'Twas thine own seeking Faustus, thank thyself." When Faustus says that he "will renounce this magic and repent," he himself in a lucid moment recognizes that repentance is still possible. And the Good Angel at once announces also that a true act of contrition followed by God's forgiveness can still occur. But continued exercise in sin is robbing Faustus of volition—"My heart is harden'd, I cannot repent." However, this too must be taken as an egocentric conclusion. No sooner does he think of holy things than all kinds of instruments for self-destruction are placed before him. But in self-revelation he gives us another sharp insight into his essential make-up:

> And long ere this I should have done the deed
> Had not sweet pleasure conquer'd deep despair.

As I have pointed out, sensuous pleasure is always Faustus' remedy for spiritual despair. He has had Homer and Orpheus sing for him. And now the very thought of former pleasure drugs his conscience:

> Why should I die then or basely despair?—
> I am resolv'd Faustus shall not repent!

It is instructive to compare Macbeth with Faustus. The former is tremendous in his spiritual agony. But the Faustus who, here and elsewhere, goes through such rapid mental and emotional gyrations is surely conceived of by his creator as of infinitely smaller dimension.

In the latter part of the same scene there is almost a replica of the pattern of the first part. Mephostophilis tells Faustus: "Thou art damn'd. Think thou of Hell!" And the magician once more characteristically blames Lucifer's servant for his plight: " 'Tis thou hast damn'd distressed Faustus' soul." And so again the protagonist is in spiritual distress. The Good Angel tells him there is still time to repent. But the Bad Angel threatens, "If thou repent, devils will tear thee in pieces." (We must remember that the obverse of love of pleasure is fear of pain.) Just as Faustus calls upon his Savior for help, Lucifer, Belzebub, and Mephostophilis enter. Lucifer appears menacing and frightening:

Faust. O, what art thou that look'st so terribly?

And after a few lines of prodding, the wretchedly irresolute hedonist once more veers and vows "never to look to Heaven!" Again the Devil gets Faustus out of his melancholy by providing him with some satisfaction of the senses—the show of the Seven Deadly Sins. Note again Marlowe's dramatic irony:

> That sight will be as pleasant to me as Paradise was to Adam the first day of his creation.

And after the show, the deluded magician in unconscious irony says, "O, how this sight doth delight my soul!"

In 3.1 at the beginning of the anti-papal scene, we have another statement by Faustus of his motivating passion:

> Sweet Mephostophilis, thou pleasest me.
> Whilst I am here on earth, let me be cloy'd
> With all the things that delight the heart of man.
> My four and twenty years of liberty
> I'll spend in pleasure and in dalliance. . . .

And in 4.3, the Horse-Courser scene, Marlowe shows the protagonist still tormented—but still capable of rapid self-delusion:

> What art thou, Faustus, but a man condemn'd to die?
> Thy fatal time draws to a final end . . .
> Despair doth drive distrust into my thoughts.
> Confound these passions with a quiet sleep.
> Tush, Christ did call the thief upon the cross!
> Then rest thee Faustus, quiet in conceit.

In the last act, Marlowe once more returns us forcefully to the serious business of his play. At the very beginning Wagner is struck by the inconsistency of his master's character. The latter has made his will and hence "means to die shortly." But, says the puzzled servant, "If death were nigh, he would not frolic thus. He's now at supper with the scholars, where there's such belly-cheer as Wagner in his life ne'er saw the like!" Thus, through the mouth of another character, the playwright shows us Faustus as still the incorrigible hedonist. The scholars wish him to show them Helen of Troy. Mephostophilis brings in the peerless dame, and the scholars are ravished. The latter leave—and *"Enter an Old Man."* The latter movingly begs Faustus to give up his wicked life. Here we have explicit statement that Faustus is still a man (and not a spirit); that he still has "an amiable soul"; that he is still capable of repentance; that if he does not change his wicked ways, his nature will become incapable of contrition; and that by "checking [his] body" he "may amend [his] soul." Faustus' reaction to the Old Man's speech

is typical. He utterly despairs, is positive of his damnation, and is about
to kill himself with a dagger which Mephostophilis provides. Thus,
in the reverse kind of egotism in which Faustus indulges when he is
conscience-stricken, he completely misses the burden of the Old Man's
message: no man's sins are too great for God to forgive. But the Old
Man cries out for him to stop, tells him that "precious grace" waits
only upon prayer for mercy. Faustus thanks the Old Man for words
that "comfort my distressed soul" and asks to be left alone to ponder
his sins. But the Old Man knows how weak the magician is:

> Faustus, I leave thee; but with grief of heart,
> Fearing the enemy of thy hapless soul.

We immediately see that the Old Man was right in his apprehensions.
Faustus is now in the toils:

> Accursed Faustus! Wretch, what hast thou done!
> I do repent, and yet I do despair:
> Hell strives with grace for conquest in my breast!
> What shall I do to shun the snares of death?

Hell strives against Heaven: despair against repentance. But as soon
as Mephostophilis arrests him for disobedience, commands him to deny
God, threatens physical pain—"or I'll in piecemeal tear thy flesh"—
the weak-willed voluptuary caves in. He "repents" (*sic!*) that he has
offended Lucifer, offers of his own volition to confirm with blood his
former vow, and—characteristically blaming another for his treason—
brutally begs Mephostophilis to torture the Old Man "With greatest
torment that our [*sic!*] Hell affords." Is this the superman whom de-
votees of the Renaissance describe?

Once more we see the familiar pattern operating. Faustus requests
the moly which will deaden his spiritual apprehension:

> One thing, good servant, let me crave of thee
> To glut the longing of my heart's desire:
> That I may have unto my paramour
> That heavenly Helen which I saw of late,
> Whose sweet embraces may extinguish clear
> Those thoughts that do dissuade me from my vow,
> And keep [the] ⟨oath⟩ I made to Lucifer.

Helen appears. Faustus delivers the famous apostrophe, "Was this the
face . . ." and leaves the stage with her.

How are we to take these lines? For the sake of bodily pleasure,
Faustus has given up the last possibility of redemption and embraced
Hell. Surely we do not even have to recognize that Helen is a succuba,
the Devil in female guise, to recognize Marlowe's point!

The next scene is that of Faustus' going down to Hell. The comment of Mephostophilis at its beginning is sharply descriptive:

> Fond worldling, now his heart blood dries with grief,
> His conscience kills it, and his laboring brain
> Begets a world of idle fantasies
> To overreach the Devil—but all in vain:
> His store of pleasures must be sauc'd with pain!

And note how admirably Marlowe shows us the kernel of this unstable, foolish worldling. The Second Scholar has asked him to repent, "mercy is infinite." Faustus replies:

> But Faustus' offense can ne'er be pardoned. The serpent that tempted Eve may be saved, but not Faustus! O, gentlemen, hear with patience and tremble not at my speeches. Though my heart pant and quiver to remember that I have been a student here these thirty years, O, would I had never seen Wittenberg, never read book.—And what wonders I have done, all Germany can witness, yea all the world!—For which Faustus hath lost both Germany and the world, yea, Heaven itself—Heaven, the seat of God, the throne of the blessed, the kingdom of joy—and must remain in Hell forever! Hell, O Hell forever! Sweet friends, what shall become of Faustus being in Hell forever?

One should not pass over lightly the exceedingly dramatic nature of this speech. The quaking Faustus is still the blatant egotist. He knows that God cannot pardon him! And in the midst of his self-reproach, lo! the basic vanity leaps forth—"And what wonders I have done, all Germany can witness, yea all the world!"

Faustus sums up his situation succinctly: "For the vain pleasure of four and twenty years hath Faustus lost eternal joy and felicity." He gave up higher values for lower. And the burden of the Good and Bad Angels who enter now is that for small pleasure the voluptuary has given up great pleasures, for small pleasures he must now endure all the horrible sensory tortures of Hell. The Bad Angel concludes, "He that loves pleasure must for pleasure fall." Such is the ironic outcome.

But the most trenchant stroke of Marlowe's pervading irony is in the famous last soliloquy. Faustus, too late, begs for time to repent, and in his agony cries out, *"O lente lente currite noctis equi!"* This is Ovid, *Amores*, I. xiii. 40. Habituated to sensual pleasure, Faustus—begging now for time to save his soul—must perforce use the words of Ovid in his mistress's arms!

Faustus: A Great Work Flawed

by J. B. Steane

If *Faustus* is a great work, it is also a flawed one. It is not merely a matter of two poor scenes and two which degenerate into nonsense, a sequence of trivial episodes and two occasions where the climax is disappointingly followed up. There is also, more seriously, a lack of sustained concentrated writing in places where one might have hoped for it, and often, by Shakespearean standards at any rate, a poverty of poetic texture. Sometimes, as one is thinking how to describe something in the play, a Shakespearean phrase comes to mind: Faustus, for instance, might be described as

> destil'd
> Almost to *Ielly* with the Act of feare.
> *(Hamlet,* I. 2)

It is a very unremarkable phrase in the richness of its context but would represent a remarkable enrichment of vocabulary in a Marlovian context. How far Marlowe is *responsible* for these shortcomings is an irrelevant query when one is concerned, as I have been, with the text as the object or fact which exists for us.

This "fact" has rarely been the critics' prime apparent interest in the play. Perhaps an exception is Mr. James Smith, whose essay in *Scrutiny*[1] was limited to certain aspects of *Faustus* as a work of art. But the prime concern seems to have been with *Faustus* as a significant phenomenon rather than a work of art. Mr. Levin's close study, for instance, appears to have as its prime concern an act of relating or connecting; that is, it seems for the most part to be interested in the text when it can be related to something outside itself, a whole body of European culture, adduced with breadth and knowledge, but involving the play more as a portent, a significance, than a work of art.

[1] VIII, 1.

This is true also of Miss Mahood's penetrating remarks in *Poetry and Humanism*. The effect of this kind of interest has been both to shrug off too lightly the flaws in the play (its "significance" remains) *and* to insulate the reader from the full force of the work (as opposed to recognition of the "phenomenon").

It is true that some of these flaws are not beyond defence. The middle section, writes Harry Levin, "is unquestionably weak. The structural weakness, however, corresponds to the anti-climax of the parable; it lays bare the gap between promise and fruition, between the bright hopes of the initial scene and the abysmal consequences of the last." There are other points of correspondence. I understand Mr. Levin to mean that these middle scenes act, in their weakness, as a gap between the first and last sections, throwing them and the contrast between them into relief. He seems, then, to be referring to the *ultimate* fruition. But the disappointment of the immediate fruition is enforced also. The "world of profit and delight" turns out, as dramatised, to be sadly trivial, even progressively trivial, and ever-less vital. There is a certain wonder in Faustus' European travel, as described by himself and the Chorus; also a certain zest about the doings in the Vatican. Both the wonder and the fun degenerate in the scene with the Emperor. The fun is at its lowest with the Horse-Courser, and wonder is practically extinguished in the Vanholt scene. So that this middle section does not exactly "lay bare" the gap between the promise of the first scene and the fruition of the last, but shows the stages between them. The scenes illustrate the growing emptiness of the way of life Faustus has chosen. That is (and must have been then to the sensitive part of the audience) the moral effect; though there is some relevance in the objection that there are better ways of presenting boredom than by being boring, or triviality than by being trivial.

It is not likely that Goethe had this sort of discussion in mind when he made that famous remark, "How greatly is it all planned." Yet these are the points that need facing in order to say it and mean anything very much by it. This dictum, like the middle section of the play, has something to be said for it, not so much by virtue of its doubtful intentions, but because, in itself and as it stands, it has point. (The intended meaning seems not to be what the modern critic would like to make it, for the adjective *gross* suggests something more like "on a large scale," great in the sense of large, rather than a qualitative judgment; and, although in English the emphasis of the sentence comes meaningfully on "planned," in German the emphasis probably falls on *gross* rather than *angelegt,* which anyway suggests "laid out" as of a park or garden, which is not really very appropriate to *Faustus*.)

The great planning, however, is plentifully in evidence. Miss Ma-

hood justifies the term by reference to the "philosophical structure";
and one might add the creation and development of character, the
working of dramatic climax, and the linking backwards and forwards,
by means open to the dramatic poet (and Marlowe is primarily that,
not a philosopher), of lines and phrases which thus gain in intensity
and relevance.

Other kinds of planning it clearly has not. Any complex interplay
of plots and characters, for example. It has the structural bareness of
the fifteenth-century *Everyman* which in several ways it resembles.
The grave dignity of that play is absent (in its mirth and knockabout
mixed with serious matter, *Faustus* is more like the normal Morality
than *Everyman* is). Moreover, Marlowe has, characteristically, reversed much in the traditional Morality pattern. *Everyman* and *Mankind,* for instance, dramatise Holy Dying and Holy Living respectively:
Faustus is about evil living and consequently desperate dying. Mankind and Everyman crawl up to their God; Faustus even in his last
hour still aspires to leap, and it can't be done. The earlier pair, in a
pilgrim's progress, climb the steep ascent of Heaven, and flights of
angels sing Everyman to his rest; Faustus, the Devil's disciple, goes
the primrose way and Hell calls with a roaring voice. But the admoni-
tions of *Everyman* are those of *Faustus*:

> The story sayth: man, in the begynnynge
> Loke well and take good heed to the endynge,
> Be you never so gay.

And in both plays, a man's soul is the stage; the forces from without
correspond to forces within, and Heaven and Hell play for the victory.

The people of the mediæval psychomachia have the representative
characters of their names. That is, they are not distinctive characters
at all, however convincingly human in their reaction to the given
situation. Faustus is an individual in spite of the tendency the morality
element has to categorise him among the "forward wits." He is inevitably one of a class or type—the young extremist, eager and buoyant,
with a brilliantly energetic, inquiring mind, intoxicated by his en-
thusiasms, heady in his dislikes, and fundamentally superficial in both.
But the character develops. After the Vatican scene, the boyish quality disappears and there is a sense of ageing. The keynote of the weak
Vanholt scene is its courtesy, and in that and the two later scenes with
the scholars it is a quieter and more mature Faustus who is admired.
As in the beginning he was placed in a relationship of youth with
age by the "sage conference" of Valdes and Cornelius, so in the last
act he is felt to be a senior man in company with the scholars. His
sheer energy has declined. "Confound these passions with a quiet
sleepe"; later the scenes with Helen have almost the quiet dignity of

an Indian summer; and his sighs in the last scene with the scholars
are those of a man whose vitality is weakened. But in all these things
he is still, partly, representative. In other respects he is a very unusual
man indeed.

He is a chaos of will and impotence. His humanism, proud and aspiring, is expressed in the lines:

> All things that mooue betweene the quiet poles
> Shalbe at my commaund, Emperours and Kings
> Are but obeyd in their seuerall prouinces;
> Nor can they raise the winde, or rend the cloudes,
> But his dominion that exceedes in this,
> Stretcheth as farre as doth the minde of man.
>
> (84–9)

"The mind of man" is the nearest thing in creation to infinity; it is
creation's crown. But it is checked by nature: the winds and clouds
are nothing in the scale of being, yet they remain as symbols of in-
tractable matter. Man is limited (this is the feeling) not by his own
nature, but by the nature of the world that encloses him. Miss Mahood
says, "Pride in man's potentialities is swiftly reversed to despair at his
limitations":

> Yet are thou still but *Faustus,* and a man.
>
> (51)

She also writes of the "extreme swings of the pendulum" in Faustus:
"contemptuous pride and incredulous despair." What sets the pendulum in motion concerns the will; here there is a fundamental instability. Faustus sees the will as the ultimate power within man, but it is a
will which at the same time he morbidly suspects to be illusory and
governed by something outside itself.

He dismisses Divinity because it seems to involve a hateful deter-
minism which denies the real freedom to "settle," "begin" and "be."
Faustus is intent, as the essential means to any worth-while end, on
asserting his will. His first speech is that of a man determined not to
run on wheels; he is to make the existentialist choice and start living.
His will may, as he implies to Mephastophilis, be boundless and
crazy. He may assert it in something like Gide's *acte gratuit*:

> Be it to make the Moone drop from her spheare,
> Or the Ocean to ouerwhelme the world.
>
> (273–4)

He might in fact will to act out Ulysses' Order speech, "and make a
soppe of all this solid Globe": "Then euery thing includes it selfe in
. . . Will."

But the rejected biblical texts also proclaimed (in their truncated form) a necessary, fated damnation. It is no accident that precisely those texts are chosen, or that Faustus should have overlooked or have deliberately and proudly set his face against that text which follows the quotation from St. John: "But if we confess our sins, he is faithful and just to forgive us our sins, and cleanse us from all un-righteousness." That is the Christian doctrine of grace, and Faustus has no conception of it. Clearly, then, in his mind, he must be damned if there is any truth in Divinity. He has made a gesture of dismissal towards Divinity and acted on the assumption that he has done more than that. But he has not in fact dismissed it from his mind at all. This lurking sense of damnation *precedes* the invocation to Mepha-stophilis, and the conviction of it precedes the formal deed with Lucifer:

> Now *Faustus* must thou needes be damnd,
> And canst thou not be saued? . . .
> To God? he loues thee not,
> The god thou seruest is thine owne appetite.
>
> (433–4, 442–3)

In this speech is expressed not only the certainty of damnation but a deep sense of sinfulness: he does not deserve God's love for he has served his appetite ("Will into Appetite"). Again, the sinfulness is not just the result of his dealings with the devil but also the cause of them: it was not his "coniuring speeches" that raised Mephastophilis, but his spiritual condition. The conviction of worthlessness and in-evitable damnation grows:

> If vnto God hee'l throwe thee downe to hell.
>
> (510)

The words of the Evil Angel strengthen it:

> Thou art a spirite, God cannot pitty thee.
>
> (624)

And the fearful echo of Faustus' own thought: "Too late." Scepticism, hope and attempted repentance all challenge this conviction in Faustus, but it is deeply embedded in his thought and emerges ulti-mately in the last speech:

> You starres that raignd at my natiuitie,
> Whose influence hath alotted death and hel . . .
>
> (1443–4)

The free-thinking Renaissance humanist only hides a traditionalism which is basically mediæval: the conservatism of Lear's Gloucester as against the bright scepticism of the "new man" Edmund.

The forces represented in this tension within the individual are deep in European civilisation, and that explains why commentators have been so much concerned with *Faustus* as a "significance." Strangely, the man whose story comes to mind as being most Faust-like in this way lived neither in the Renaissance nor the Middle Ages, but in the "Age of Reason." Cowper's biography contains a terrible latter-day psychomachia: "His bedroom was every night the battle-ground of a struggle between good and evil spirits, and . . . in the end the evil always vanquished the good, and then 'Bring him out!' they would cry, 'bring him out!'." Cowper was convinced of his dam-nation: "On the night of 24 February he had a dream. What it pre-cisely was no one knows; but in it amid circumstances of unspeakable horror, he heard from the lips of God himself the certain and irrevo-cable sentence of his damnation. . . . Within the centre of his con-sciousness remained unaltered the conviction that he was damned, that every day he passed brought him a day nearer to an eternity of torment; and he had fixed his eyes exclusively on such things as could still give him pleasure, had laboriously derived from them the whole elaborate scheme of occupation and habit and amusement which was his mode of life, in order to distract himself from the frightful fate that awaited him." [2] This is from what another writer has described as "the saddest and sweetest life in English literature!" [3] Here are two of Cowper's own utterances, the first from an early poem (*Hatred and Vengeance*):

> Damned below Judas; more abhorred than he was,
> Who for a few pence sold his holy Master!
> Twice betrayed, Jesus me, the last delinquent,
>   Deems the profanest.

And the second from his diary:

> Friday, Nov. 16th . . . Dreamt that in a state of the most insupportable misery, I looked through the window of a strange room, being all alone, and saw preparations being made for my execution. That it was about four days distant and that then I was destined to suffer everlasting martyrdom in the fire, my body being prepared for the purpose and my dissolution made a thing impossible. Rose overwhelmed with infinite despair, and came down into the study, execrating the day I was born with inexpressible bitterness.

This "sweet, sad life" is, in this, not unlike what Marlowe presents us with in *Faustus*. Conscious of the Romantic heresy, one wonders whether it has anything in common with Marlowe's own.

---

[2] Quotations from *The Stricken Deer* by Lord David Cecil.
[3] George Sampson, *The Concise Cambridge History of English Literature.*

The involvement of the author in his work is, of course, much debated. John Bakeless "feels an autobiographical touch, feels it keenly too." Miss Josephine Preston Peabody, quoted by Bakeless, had no doubt about it. She makes the Marlowe of her play cry: "I am the man, the devil and the soul." Others imply it in their judgments. Michel Poirier writes: "That more or less conscious distortion of the Christian doctrine is rather to be ascribed to the author's nature, to his narrow logic, to his incapacity to understand the grandeur and beauty of the message of the Gospel." That is to make Marlowe "the man" at least, and virtually "the devil" as well. Critics in the opposing camp include Miss Mahood, James Smith and Roy Battenhouse.

A decision here depends partly on the attitude one already has to questions of this kind, and partly on the amount of weight one allows such biographical evidence as the Baines note. With P. H. Kocher, I take the note seriously. As Faustus had used "such meanes whereby he [was] in danger to be damnd," so (the evidence suggests) had Marlowe. It does not follow that Marlowe is making a personal recantation as some have thought, or that he had no more idea of grace than Faustus had (as Poirier implies), or that the play is essentially a sermon on the explicit "moral" of the Epilogue. But when Miss Mahood says that "In his tragic heroes he has embodied the spiritual adventures of his own generation, as he observed them," one has to add that as he was himself "of his own generation" he probably, like his introspective Faustus, observed his own spiritual adventures with particular closeness. He does in fact seem to me to be "giving of his own substance," as Professor Waldock says of Milton[4]; and this does not open him to Dr. Leavis's charge which he makes—justly, I think—against Milton, of failing to depersonalise "the relevant interests and impulses of his private life."

For if "his own substance" is there, and if the biographical evidence for supposing this is true, then Marlowe achieved a rare degree of detachment. The Marlowe of the Baines note and the tales is treated with little respect. The knight in the Emperor's court, for instance, is in some ways an enlightened freethinker. He will not accept Faustus on authority: "Ifaith he lookes much like a coniurer." That, according to the Baines note, was very much Marlowe's attitude to the reputation of Moses. The knight is contemptuous of the conjuring, and smart in the style of his commenting. In his promise to the Emperor, Faustus has allowed himself a fairly generous logical loop-hole. The knight observes it and says "Ifaith thats iust nothing at all." One might suppose this sceptical intelligence to be congenial to Marlowe, but in fact the knight is humiliated. This scene may not be Marlowe's own,

---

[4] *Paradise Lost and Its Critics* (Cambridge, 1947).

but the same is true of Faustus himself in a scene which is certainly authentic. He too is a freethinker with advanced notions: "Come, I thinke hell's a fable." And later:

> Thinkst thou that *Faustus* is so fond, to imagine,
> That after this life there is any paine?
> Tush, these are trifles and meere olde wiues tales. (565–7)

And:

> This word damnation terrifies not him,
> For he confounds hell in *Elizium*.
> His ghost be with the olde Philosophers.[5]   (294–6)

These are all in spirit like the Marlowe of the Baines note, willing men "not to be afeard of bugbeares and hobgoblins" and persuading them "to Atheism." This boastfully independent freethinking always carries with it a dramatic irony in the play, and provokes the bitterly ironical comment of Mephastophilis: "I, thinke so still, till experience change thy minde."

Perhaps it would seem that Marlowe could not have the views attributed to him by the Baines note and at the same time hold them up to irony and humiliation in the play. But it surely is possible, understandable and moving. It would only argue in Marlowe a division and uncertainty like that he dramatises with this characteristic see-saw or wave motion in Faustus. Indeed if there is any truth in his reputation as it has come down to us, some such division is surely inevitable. However firmly a man believed with his reason that traditional religion is essentially superstition, he must also, in his soul, have felt that traditional wisdom affirming the religion could not be so utterly mistaken. The Baines note shows a nonconformist, confident in his attack and almost heroic in his boldness. But the weight of ages cannot be shaken off, and if the ages are not wrong then the free-thinker must be. If he is wrong, they are right; and if they are right there is pain after this life; and for those who abjure the Scriptures, exercising their pitiful intelligence where a blind understanding is required, the ten thousand doors of hell wait ajar. The Marlowe who wrote *Faustus* need not have renounced publicly or privately the non-conformity of the Baines note, but he must have known doubts and fears of an agonising kind. Such a tension would involve a very Faust-like instability.

Instability is fundamental in the play, as a theme and a character-istic. *Faustus* is a play of violent contrasts within a rigorous structural

[5] J. C. Maxwell (*Notes and Queries,* CXCIV) has noted the identity of the last line with a saying attributed to the Arabic philosopher Averroes, expressing his hostility to Christianity.

unity. Hilarity and agony, seriousness and irresponsibility: even on the most cautious theories of authorship, Marlowe is responsible at times for all these extremes. This artistic instability matches the instability of the hero. The extremes of optimism and depression, enthusiasm and hatred, commitment to Hell and aspiration to Heaven, pride and shame: these are the swings of the pendulum in Faustus' world, and they are reflected by the sickening to-and-fro motion of the verse— an ambivalence first felt in the Prologue's "forme of *Faustus* fortunes good or bad." But this to-and-fro of extremes is not the only movement in the play. The other movement (and this seems to me fundamental in Marlowe's career as a writer, as it is in this play) is one of *shrinkage*. Faustus stands on his own two feet, a proud thing in creation, as he conjures in his lusty grove; but in the end, he cowers and hides, wishing his manhood to be shrunk to the stature of a brutish beast and finally to that of the lowest, least individual thing in the creation he once thought to dominate. He is bent and shrunk not merely by his contact with evil, but because in the first place he would not bend and shrink submissively to the will of the powers that shape the world. Man has to crawl between heaven and hell. In *Tamburlaine* that space seemed so ample that he could strut wonderfully and challenge the other worlds to match his splendour. In *Faustus* this world (and Faustus like a millionaire tourist has "done it all") yields less. In the other plays it is to yield less still.

The Orthodoxy of *Faustus*

by L. C. Knights

Criticism, we know, should beware of interpreting particular works in the light of general notions imputed, on various grounds, to their author. *Dr. Faustus* is important for what it is—a work of art in which the desire for effortless and unlimited power is subjected to the scrutiny of a powerful mind—and not merely as a document in the history of Marlowe's religious beliefs. In attempting a total estimate of the dramatist, however, it is impossible not to be puzzled by the relation between the orthodoxy so emphatically asserted in the play and the opinions attributed to Marlowe both by Kyd and Baines. And the fact that there *is* a puzzle may throw some light on the play itself.

Marlowe's persistent concern with religion was certainly not confined to exposing the gulf between the beliefs and the practices of professing Christians, and Kocher is right to insist on that fundamental aspect of Marlowe's thought. It is doubtful, however, whether he was the dedicated rationalist that Kocher makes him out to be. In the documents to which I have referred there are strictly rational arguments and objections to the fundamentalist strain in contemporary Christian thought, but there are also merely exasperated assertions of anti-Christian attitudes. And although the latter may be explained in part by the failure of his Christian contemporaries to meet him—as a Hooker could have met him—with more than dogmatic assertions, there is a residue of what seems like mere obsessive blasphemy. Referring to some of Marlowe's more outrageous statements, Kyd said, "he would so suddenly take slight occasion to slip [them] out." "Almost into every company he cometh," said Baines, "he persuades men to atheism." In both statements there is the suggestion of a compulsive need, and although it would be useless and impertinent to try to trace this compulsion to its sources, it may nevertheless offer a clue to the ambivalent effect of *Dr. Faustus*.

"The Orthodoxy of Faustus*" (Editor's title). From* Further Explorations *by L. C. Knights (London: Chatto & Windus Ltd., 1965; Stanford, California: Stanford University Press, 1965), pp. 94–98. Copyright © 1965 by L. C. Knights. Reprinted by permission of the publishers.*

No one who studies the play with any care can subscribe to the view that Marlowe damns Faustus unwillingly, either as a concession to orthodoxy or because of a final failure of nerve. No one writes poetry of the order of Faustus's last terrible soliloquy without being wholly engaged,[1] and more than in any other of his plays Marlowe shows that he knows what he is doing. From the superbly presented dis-ingenuousness of the opening soliloquy, in which Faustus dismisses the traditional sciences with a series of quibbles, Marlowe is making a sustained attempt to present as it really is the perverse and infantile desire for enormous power and immediate gratifications.

> O what a world of profit and delight,
> Of power, of honour and omnipotence,
> Is promis'd to the studious artizan!
> All things that move between the quiet poles
> Shall be at my command.[2]

However deeply Marlowe may have been versed in demonology it is unlikely that he took very seriously the business of "Lines, circles, letters and characters." Baudelaire says somewhere, *"Tout homme qui n'accepte pas les conditions de la vie vend son âme,*[3] and a modern writer, James Baldwin, "Everything in a life depends on how that life accepts its limits." [4] It is in the light of such remarks that we should see the pact with the devil and the magic: they serve as dramatic representations of the desire to ignore that "rightness of limitation," which, according to Whitehead, "is essential for growth of reality." [5] Marlowe—the overreacher—was only too familiar with that desire, and the turning on himself—on the self of *Tamburlaine,* Part I—is a measure of his genius.

[1] A point developed by James Smith in a notable essay, "Marlowe's *Dr. Faustus*" in *Scrutiny,* VIII, June 1939.

[2] If this is not sufficiently placed by the immediate context, there is the implicit comment in Faustus's words to Valdes and Cornelius (complete only in the A text) which editors have strangely found obscure:

> Know that your words have won me at the last
> To practise magic and concealed arts:
> Yet not your words only, but *mine own fantasy,*
> *That will receive no object.* . . .

Marlowe also slips in a hint or two that Faustus's prowess as a scholar had con-tained an element of self-inflation and aggression: his "subtle syllogisms Gravell'd the pastors of the German church" etc. (I, i, 113 ff.); and one can almost hear the scholar's pride with which he "was wont to make our schools ring with *sic probo*" (I, ii, 1–2).

[3] Quoted by Enid Starkie, *Rimbaud,* p. 123.

[4] *Nobody Knows my Name: More Notes of a Native Son,* p. 145.

[5] A. N. Whitehead, *Religion in the Making* (Meridian Books), p. 146.

Some such intention as I have described, the intention of coming to terms with a corrupting day-dream, determines the main structural lines and the great passages of *Dr. Faustus*. But few even of the play's warmest admirers claim that it lives in the imagination as an entirely satisfying and consistent whole. Interest flags and is fitfully revived. And although the scenes in which Faustus's power is exhibited in such imbecile ways may be defended as presenting the gross stupidity of sin, this always feels to me, in the reading, as an explanation that has been thought up. With one or two exceptions, Faustus's capers represent an escape from seriousness and full realization—not simply on Faustus's part but on Marlowe's: and what they pad out is a crucial gap in the play's imaginative structure. For where, we may ask, are the contrasting positives against which Faustus's misdirection of his energies could be measured?

With this we return once more to the unresolved conflicts, the intrusive subjectivity, in terms of which it seems necessary to explain this remarkable play, as they are necessary to explain the obvious failures. It is not merely that—unlike Macbeth—Faustus has no vision of the life-giving values against which he has offended: Marlowe doesn't grasp them either. And you have the uneasy feeling that Faustus's panic fear of hell is not only the inevitable result of a wilful, self-centred denial of life. It is as though Marlowe himself felt guilt about *any* of his assertive drives (understandably enough, since they were tied up with his regressions), and conceived of religion not in terms of a growth into freedom and reality but as binding and oppressing.

We may put this in another way. I have said that in some important respects Marlowe's creative fantasy did not meet sufficient resistance— the kind of resistance that is necessary for the production of the highest kind of energy, which is at once affirmation, growth and understanding. In *Dr. Faustus* the resistance is, as it were, externalized. The anarchic impulse (the Ganymede-Tamburlaine fantasy) collides with a prohibition. Because what is prohibited and rebuked in this play is indeed a denial of life, and because the rebuke is charged with the full force of that other self of Marlowe's which appears so fitfully in the other plays, the result is poetry of very great power indeed. But even in the last great despairing speech, where almost overpowering feeling moulds the language in a way in which it had never been moulded before, the reader's submission is, I suggest, of a different order from the submission one gives to the greatest art, where a sense of freedom is the concomitant of acceptance of reality, however painful this may be.

If this is indeed so, it does something to explain how the orthodoxy of *Dr. Faustus* and the animus against religion in the Baines document and elsewhere could be harboured simultaneously. It also helps to explain the diametrically opposed views to be found among the critics of the play. It seems to me that those who see the final soliloquy as the logical culmination of the play's action are right; and that those who see a more or less deliberate suppression of Marlowe's sympathy for his hero, in order to bring about an orthodox dénouement, are wrong. But the latter are in fact responding to an unresolved emotional quality that lies behind the rational structure of the play.

PART TWO

View Points

Francis Macdonald Cornford

Certain features which survived in Greek tragedy suggest that we
should look back to a type somewhat resembling the mediaeval mystery and some of the earliest modern dramas, such as *Everyman,*
which are like the mystery in being religious performances and in the
element of allegorical abstraction. Their effect, due in part to each
of these features, may be described as *symbolic. Everyman* is a sermon
made visible. To watch it is like watching the pastime called "living
chess," in which the pieces are men and women, but the man who
is dressed like a bishop is nothing more than a chessman who happens
to be automatic. He has not the episcopal character; his dress is a
disguise with nothing behind it; his words, if he spoke, would be the
speech of a parrot. And so it is with *Everyman.* The persons are not
persons at all, but *personae*, masks, symbols, the vehicles of abstract
ideas. They do not exist, and could not be conceived as existing, in
real space and time. They have no human characters, no inward mo-
tives, no life of their own. Everyman, as his name is meant to show,
is in fact not *a* man, but Man, the universal.

The main development of modern drama shows, in one of its aspects,
the process by which this symbolic method gives way to the realistic.
The process consists in the gradual filling in of the human being behind the mask, till the humanity is sufficiently concrete and vital to
burst the shell and step forth in solid flesh and blood. The symbol
comes to contain a type of character; the type is particularized into
a unique individual. The creature now has an independent status and
behaviour of its own. Every gesture and every word must be such as
would be used by an ordinary human being with the given character
in the given situation. Once created, the personality is an original
centre; it cannot be made to do what we please or to utter our
thoughts. In some such terms as these a modern novelist or playwright
will speak of his characters; and it is thus that they appear to us.

Now we can observe a certain intermediate stage in which these
two methods, the symbolic and the realistic, are balanced in antago-

From Thucydides Mythhistoricus *by Francis Macdonald Cornford (London:
Edward Arnold Ltd., 1907; New York: Humanities Press Inc., 1965), pp. 141–43.
Copyright © 1907 by Edward Arnold Ltd. Reprinted by permission of the pub-
lishers.*

nism, so as to produce a curious effect of tension and incoherency. A good instance is Marlowe's *Faustus*. Faustus himself occupies the central plane; he is a living man, but still imprisoned in a symbolical type. The intrusion of humanity has gone far enough to disturb the abstract effect, and it reacts on some of the persons in the play who ought to be purely symbolic. Lucifer, it is true, is kept apart and remains non-human; but Mephistophilis oscillates in our imagination between the ideal and reality, with a distressing result. Again, on a lower level than Faustus there is yet another grade of persons, in contrast with whom he shows up as heroic and ideal. These are the vintner, the horse-courser, and other pieces of common clay picked out of a London alley; they belong to a different world, and we feel that they could no more communicate with the tragic characters than men can talk with angels.[1] Thus there are in this one play four sets or orders of persons: (1) the purely abstract and *symbolic,* such as Lucifer, who only appears on an upper stage at certain moments, and takes no part in the action; (2) the *intermediate,* for instance Mephistophilis, who ought to be symbolic, but treads the lower stage, a cowled enigma,[2] horrible because at moments he ceases to be symbolic without becoming human; (3) the *heroic* or tragic: Faustus, who is an ideal half realized, hanging together on its own plane; (4) the *real*: common mortals who would attract no attention in Fleet Street.

The Greek drama, although in the detail of historical development it started at a different point from the modern, and followed another course, seems, nevertheless, to pass through a phase analogous to that which we have just described.

Paul H. Kocher

Within this framework, which it has voluntarily imposed upon itself, the spirit of Marlowe's iconoclasm struggles fitfully to burst free. For example, when the two angels prompt Faustus,

From Christopher Marlowe: A Study of His Thought, Learning, and Character *by Paul H. Kocher (Chapel Hill, North Carolina: The University of North Carolina Press, 1946; New York: Russell & Russell, 1961), pp. 114–16. Copyright 1946 by the University of North Carolina Press. Reprinted by permission of the author and the publisher.*

[1] We hope it is true that Marlowe did not write the comic scenes; but we are only concerned with the effect of the play as it stands.

[2] In the Elizabethan Stage Society's representation Mephistophilis is cowled and *his face is never seen.* The effect is indescribably horrible. At certain moments in Greek Tragedy the mask must have produced a somewhat similar effect, though the familiarity of the convention would make it much less in degree. The longing to see the actor's face, when his words are enigmatic, is almost enough to drive a modern spectator insane.

> *Faustus.* Contrition, prayer, repentance—what of these?
> *Good Ang.* O, they are means to bring thee unto heaven!
> *Bad Ang.* Rather illusions, fruits of lunacy,
>   That make them foolish that do use them most,
>
>   (II, i, 17–20)

we know that the Good Angel is doctrinally right. But we also know that the Bad Angel is speaking for Marlowe himself, who, according to Thomas Kyd, used to "gybe at praiers" and to "iest at the devine scriptures."

*   *   *

Again, Faustus' insistence that "Hell's a fable" recalls the statement of Richard Baines that Marlowe "perswades men to Atheism willing them not to be afeared of bugbeares and hobgoblins." And so with other sallies by Faustus, the Bad Angel, or Mephistophilis against the Christian scheme.[1]

There is also a class of what might be called silent protests against the official Christianity of the play. Theologically speaking, Helen of Troy is only a fleshly wanton who decoys Faustus from the way of salvation. Yet Faustus' passion for her glows with some of Marlowe's most transcendent poetry. She is a symbol of the ideal of beauty of pagan Greece, well loved by Marlowe. In like manner, all the lucubrations, the discontents, the giant ambitions of Faustus in the first act are authoritatively condemned as evil because they denote his approaching fall. Yet the verse is exultant and the ideas and emotions are the same as those which animate Tamburlaine, Barabas, and the rest of Marlowe's great creations, and hence in all probability animated the poet himself.

Nevertheless, an important qualification must be added. It is an error to suppose that the highest poetry of the play is limited to the passages of rebellion. Surely there has seldom been more noble expression of the sense of failure and the pain of everlasting banishment from God than that of the lost demon, Mephistophilis:

> Why, this is hell, nor am I out of it:
> Think'st thou that I, that saw the face of God,
> And tasted the eternal joys of heaven,
> Am not tormented with ten thousand hells,
> In being depriv'd of everlasting bliss?
> O, Faustus, leave these frivolous demands,
> Which strikes a terror to my fainting soul.
>
>   (I, iii, 78–84)

---

[1] E.g. Faustus' malicious perversion of Christ's dying words, "Consummatum est," to the signing of his bargain with Mephistophilis (II, i, 74) is typical Marlovian gibing. And the derision of divinity in Act I is quite of a piece with Marlowe's commentaries on Scripture as reported by Baines and others.

Scarcely less eloquent are his later words:

> Hell hath no limits, nor is circumscrib'd
> In one self place; but where we are is hell,
> And where hell is, there must we ever be: . . .
>
> (II, i, 122–24)

Any rounded analysis of Marlowe's reactions to Christianity must emphatically record that this thought of hell as exile from God is able to touch deep places in his soul.

Clifford Leech

The Elizabethan playhouse, the Reformation, the formulation of practical politics that we associate with Machiavelli—these all united in taking away from the Renaissance temper something of fineness. And perhaps because the dream of human greatness was less golden, was snatched from under the eyes of the reformers, was with difficulty harnessed with a delight in political intrigue, was expressed in the still primitive theatrical terms of the 1580's, it was less enduring than Italy had known it. Even in *Tamburlaine* itself, the defection of Calyphas in Part II, his wanton truancy from his father's battles, raises awkward questions. His preference for a game of cards over witnessing yet another of his father's victories is so obviously sensible when the spectators themselves have been sated with Tamburlaine's long line of triumphs; his brutal execution at his father's hands therefore seems to hint that Marlowe was growing weary of his own dream, would be ill-content with a repetition. If *Faustus* is Marlowe's next play, it is significant that there the aspirations of the individual are given to us in a morality-framework, that there is an uneasy balance between orthodoxy of religious belief and antinomianism. Later Marlowe was to turn to the more orthodox view of things, and in *Edward II*, *The Jew of Malta* and *The Massacre at Paris* there are many assertions of the sacredness of "degree": the thirst for power is shown in the Jew and Mortimer and the Guise only to be reprobated. It is as if Marlowe had at least partially abandoned the worship of man for the worship of divine decree.

But if the splendour of earthly aspiration grew tarnished in Marlowe's hands, it was indeed a crumbling idol for the Jacobeans. Chap-

From Shakespeare's Tragedies and Other Studies in Seventeenth Century Drama *by Clifford Leech (New York: Oxford University Press, 1950), pp. 38–39. Copyright © 1950 by Clifford Leech. Reprinted by permission of Chatto & Wintus Ltd. and Oxford University Press, Inc.*

man's Bussy tells us that advancement comes because it must and not because we will it, that great place brings greater vulnerability and closer contact with the antics of the court; Jonson parodies the Renaissance man in Sir Epicure Mammon; men are the stars' tennis-balls, flies at the mercy of the wanton gods, asses to be led by the nose, players strutting at the playwright's beck, bodies that rot into dust and souls driven in a black storm. Yet, just as the notion of "degree" underlies the Jacobean cosmology, so the Renaissance dream of greatness is the necessary foundation for the tragic heroes of the time. The dramatists inherited a cult of stoicism from Seneca, but it is not for their imperturbability that we admire Lear and Othello and Hamlet: in the end, it is true, they learn to stand up to Fortune's blows and to go out with dignity and a conventional gesture of resignation; but we must remember that Macbeth dies in despair, Othello in terrible remorse, and Lear with his nerves stretched beyond breaking-point by his hope that Cordelia may yet live.

Michel Poirier

However justified his reputation as a free-thinker may have been, Marlowe has refrained from making any important alterations in the religious element of the legend. Yet Faustus' behavior towards the supernatural sets the modern reader a problem that probably did not exist for the Elizabethan spectator. At the beginning, Faustus is an unbeliever in the play as well as in the English prose story. His analytic, critical attitude is that of Marlowe himself. If there be a life to come, he says, it is the Elysium the Ancients speak of. As a matter of fact, he does not believe in everlasting life; for him, God and heaven are but fond imaginings. How can he then seriously think of resorting to witchcraft? Yet he listens carefully to the advice of his friends who are addicted to it, draws signs and utters formulae in order to conjure up spirits. In fact, he behaves not as a modern rationalist but as a man of his own age. His atheism, like Marlowe's, is shaken by the consensus of opinion of those among whom he lives. Who knows, after all, whether there be no dreams in the sleep of death, no God in heaven? And yet when the existence of a supernatural reality has been clearly established by two apparitions of Mephistophilis, he persists in believing that "hell's a fable." To acknowledge his grievous mistake at once might be too painful to his

From Christopher Marlowe by Michel Poirier (London: Chatto & Windus Ltd., 1950), pp. 138-39. Copyright © 1950 by Michel Poirier. Reprinted by permission of the publisher.

pride as a philosopher. Yet he is strangely deficient in logic when he fails to draw from such apparitions the conclusions they inevitably lead to. In demonstrating the existence of the devil, has he not thereby demonstrated that of God with the same degree of certainty? He reminds us of Huysmans, who reached Christian faith through occultism and his belief in hell. It is true that Faustus will soon return to the faith of his childhood, but his conversion—if we may venture to give that name to a revulsion of belief which carries with it no alteration in his conduct—has an emotional, not an intellectual origin; it is not the result of his reflections but a conseqeunce of his terror before the fate he has chosen.

Is this rediscovered faith that of a Roman Catholic or of a Protestant? The question admits of no definite answer. The Good and Evil Angels who stand by his side belong of course to the Catholic tradition, as well as the sign of the cross which he acknowledges as an exorcism. Both the Good Angel and the Old Man tell Faustus that it is never too late to repent, that he may at any moment receive the grace of God and be saved if he only prays for it. This attitude may be that of a Roman Catholic or a moderate Protestant, not of a Calvinist. On the other hand, the solitude of his soul *in articulo mortis,* the absence of any possible intercession are specifically Protestant features. Besides, he pours mockery upon "papism" and especially upon the religious orders.[2]

F. P. Wilson

Recent critics have pointed out how Faustus is cheated by the devil's promises, how he sells eternity for a toy. He asks for a wife, but his request is evaded, for he can never have a wife. He puts the question "Who made the world?" and receives no answer. "Villain," he cries to Mephostophilis, "have I not bound thee to tell me any thing"; and is answered: "Ay, that is not against our kingdom: this is. Thou art damned; think thou of hell." But there is a more dreadful deceit in the requests which he *is* granted. Nowhere is this more apparent than in the two appearances of Helen. Upon these appearances Marlowe lavishes all the magnificence at his command of richness of association and cadence, whether at her first appearance—

From Marlowe and the Early Shakespeare *by F. P. Wilson (Oxford: Clarendon Press, 1953), pp. 79–81. Reprinted by permission of the Clarendon Press, Oxford.*

[2] I. iii. 27–8 and III. i. 55–6 (text A); TB 260–1 and 854–5. An interesting study of religious thought in *Doctor Faustus* may be found in Paul H. Kocher's *Christopher Marlowe,* ch. V.

No marvel though the angry Greeks pursued
With ten years' war the rape of such a queen,
Whose heavenly beauty passeth all compare—

or in the famous apostrophe at her second appearance. But Helen is
the anodyne to deaden the anguish of his fears, and the beauty has a
terrible irony. This is still true even if we do not accept the view that
Helen is a succuba and that in his union with her Faustus has committed the sin of demoniality and sealed his damnation. If that had
been the dramatists' intention, they would, I think, have made it
more explicit. It is true, however, that before Faustus's union with
Helen the Old Man does not despair of his salvation and that after
it he does. But the Old Man was taken over from *The Damnable Life*
not by Marlowe but by a collaborator. In Marlowe's share of the play
Faustus seals his damnation when he seals with his blood the deed
by which he gives body and soul to the devil. Having done that he
has become a "spirit," and "spirit" in this play always means an evil
spirit. "Thou art a spirit; God cannot pity thee," says the Bad Angel.
Prompted by the Good Angel Faustus is conscious that even if he is
a devil God may yet pity him if he repents; but the Bad Angel has
the last word: "Ay, but Faustus never shall repent"; and Faustus knows
this to be true: "My heart is hardened, I cannot repent."

Madeleine Doran

The debate stemming from the morality play had this advantage
over the debate on purely academic questions: it allowed of a genuine,
not a specious or even merely conventional solution. When the debate
is between some form of good and evil, obviously the right choice can
only be of the good; if it is of the evil, tragedy must follow, as in
Faustus or *Macbeth*. The morality play itself and romantic comedy or
tragi-comedy mitigate the harshness of a wrong choice by allowing an
escape if a change of heart and a reversal of choice come in time, as
in *Mankind* or in *Measure for Measure* or in *The Winter's Tale*. But
tragedy keeps its inexorability and its irony by making its reversals of
choice, as in *Coriolanus,* always too late. In any case, the impasse created by the presentation of opposing points of view may be broken
only by genuine choice.

The issue may be simple and the right way evident, if unattractive,

From Endeavors of Art: A Study of Form in Elizabethan Drama *by Madeleine
Doran (Madison, Wisconsin: University of Wisconsin Press, 1954), p. 316. Reprinted
with permission of the copyright owners, the Regents of the University of Wisconsin.*

as in the appeals to Faustus of the Good Angel and of the Old Man,
or as in Macbeth's clear-sighted apprehension of "the deep damnation"
of his killing Duncan. These are tragedies in which a man knowing the
good chooses the evil. Or the issue may be between actions neither of
which is simply good nor simply evil; good and evil appear as different
faces of the same thing. Then we have arrived at such great moral
dilemmas as are faced by Brutus and Hamlet and Coriolanus. Here,
moral ambiguity lies in the nature of things corruptible, and is the
source of tragic irony.

Irving Ribner

The only one of Marlowe's plays which is cast in a deliberately
Christian context is *Doctor Faustus*, perhaps also the most difficult of
his plays to come to terms with, for of the two inadequate texts which
have come down to us only a small part can be from the pen of
Marlowe. What follows here is based upon the reconstruction by Sir
Walter Greg, which must remain our most reliable guide.[1] It is obvious
that *Doctor Faustus* is a play about human damnation and that the
contrary alternative of salvation in specifically Christian terms is always present in the dramatic context, but this need not mean that
Marlowe had returned to Christian belief when he wrote this play
any more than his authorship of *Dido* need indicate that he was ever
a pagan Greek. Christian doctrine was one of Marlowe's most vital
concerns throughout his career. Only in *Dido,* of all his plays, is it
not an important issue. Kocher has argued that much of his dramatic
activity may be explained as a struggle against the theological training
of his youth: "However desperate his desire to be free, he was bound
to Christianity by the surest of chains—hatred mingled with reluctant
longing and fascination much akin to fear" (p. 119). The damnation of
Faustus could be taken by the Elizabethan audience, as it no doubt
was, as a perfectly orthodox warning to sinners, an exemplum in the

From "Marlowe's 'Tragicke Glasse'" by Irving Ribner, in Essays on Shakespeare
and Elizabethan Drama in Honor of Hardin Craig, ed. Richard Hosley (Columbia,
Missouri: University of Missouri Press, 1962; London: Routledge & Kegan Paul
Ltd., 1962), pp. 108–10. Copyright © 1962 by the Curators of the University of
Missouri. Reprinted by permission of the publishers.

[1] *The Tragical History of the Life and Death of Doctor Faustus: A Conjectural
Reconstruction* (1950). Greg's date of 1592–3 (argued in his parallel-text edition,
1950, of the quartos of 1604 and 1616) seems to be generally accepted. That
Faustus is Marlowe's latest play had been argued on bibliographical grounds by
F. S. Boas, *Christopher Marlowe* (1940), pp. 203–4.

medieval manner delineating what the church held to be the mental state of the damned and dwelling at last upon all of the physical horrors of the soul's being carried off through the traditional Hell-mouth.

Marlowe may well have known Nathaniel Woodes's morality play, *The Conflict of Conscience,* and he may even have known the story on which that play was based, the despair and death of Francesco Spiera, an Italian Protestant who had renounced his faith.[2] But Marlowe's *Doctor Faustus* is not a Christian morality play, for it contains no affirmation of the goodness or justice of the religious system it depicts with such accuracy of detail. It is, rather, a protest against this system, which it reveals as imposing a limitation upon the aspirations of man, holding him in subjection and bondage, denying him at last even the comfort of Christ's blood, and dooming him to the most terrible destruction. The religion of the play is a Christianity from which, as Michel Poirier has pointed out (*Christopher Marlowe,* 1951, p. 141), Christ is strangely missing.

There is a terrible warning for humanity in the final chorus:

> *Faustus* is gone, regard his hellish fall
> Whose fiendful fortune may exhort the wise,
> Onely to wonder at vnlawful things,
> Whose deepenesse doth intise such forward wits,
> To practise more than heauenly power permits.
>
> (1481–5)

The price of aspiration, of seeking to probe beyond the ordinary limits of man, is death in its most horrible form. If the progress of Doctor Faustus is, as Miss Gardner has written (p. 47), "from a proud philosopher, master of all human knowledge, to a trickster, to a slave of phantoms, to a cowering wretch," this is not to say that the order of things which decrees such human deterioration as the price of aspiration beyond arbitrary limits is affirmed by Marlowe as a good or just one. The play does not preach a pious submission to divine law. It is a terribly pessimistic statement of the futility of human aspiration. In this play Marlowe is using a Christian view of Heaven and Hell in a vehicle of protest which is essentially anti-Christian.

[2] This has been suggested by Lily B. Campbell, *"Doctor Faustus:* A Case of Conscience," *PMLA,* 67 (1952), 219–39. Miss Campbell sees the play as a tragedy of despair in the medieval theological sense of refusal to accept the mercy of God. For similar Christian interpretations of the play, see M. M. Mahood, *Poetry and Humanism* (1950), pp. 67–74; Helen Gardner, "Milton's 'Satan' and the Theme of Damnation in Elizabethan Tragedy," *English Studies,* 1 (London, 1948), 46–66; and Leo Kirschbaum, "Marlowe's *Faustus:* A Reconsideration," *RES,* 19 (1943), 225–41.

Nicholas Brooke

If *Tamburlaine* is obviously different from *The Jew of Malta,* that in its turn is in many ways unlike *Dr. Faustus,* which is a more radical experiment. For *The Jew,* a play about society and politics, the sphere of the Machiavel, Marlowe revived the form of *Cambises*; for *Faustus,* about mankind in the universe, he went to the religious morality itself, and fulfilled more richly than ever all the ambivalences the form offered him. *Faustus* is supremely a play that has been distorted by wilful pre-conceptions about what it ought to be. Basically, the complaint made about it amounts to this: that it embarks on the tragic narrative of Faustus' career, invites us to see him as a tragic hero, and then deviates bewilderingly into slapstick with a horse-courser, a Pope, and an Emperor. In a sense the opening chorus seems to invite this expectation; true, it dismisses heroic war and love as themes, but it goes on:

> Only this, gentles—we must now perform
> The form of Faustus' fortunes, good or bad.
>
> (l. 7)

It might be pressing that a bit hard to remark that it is the *form* which is good or bad, not simply the fortunes; but in any case, the expectation of narrative we attach to these words is *our* expectation, based on experience of three centuries of the development of the novel. A slight acquaintance with Elizabethan fiction, whether at the level of courtly romance or popular jest-book, will immediately remind us that their notion of "story" was much more devious. But the reference here need not be so vague—the Chorus continues:

> And now to patient judgements we appeal,
> And speak for Faustus in his infancy.

Which sets the form of Faustus' fortunes firmly in a morality of the Seven Ages of Man—or rather, since this is obviously the point of the earlier disclaimer of heroic status—of mankind. The comparison is, I think, enlightening so long as I am not misunderstood to claim direct connection with the old play. The only morality to which explicit reference may be suspected is *The Conflict of Conscience,* but that was a poor specimen of the genre, and Marlowe's knowledge was obviously

From "Marlowe the Dramatist" by Nicholas Brooke, in Elizabethan Theatre (Stratford-upon-Avon Studies *9*), *eds. John Russell Brown and Bernard Harris (London: Edward Arnold [Publishers] Ltd., 1966), pp. 98–100. Copyright © 1966 by Edward Arnold (Publishers) Ltd. Reprinted by permission of the publisher.*

wider. I have no reason to suggest Marlowe knew *Mankind* itself, but he certainly knew the type. Nothing in *Mankind* offends Christian doctrine outwardly, and the idiotic farce of poor Mankind's flirtation with the devil ultimately justifies the unbendingly severe forgiveness he receives. Yet the play is alive, if not actually with protestantism (it sounds like Lollardry at times), at least with protestation: Mercy as a feudal overlord is a strange and striking image; and Mercy and Mischief as born brothers, to whom the helpless image of ourselves is committed in sad if silly slavery, is a very suggestive conception. Marlowe's Lucifer and Christ are not brothers; but they are closely related images of submission for Faustus. His oscillation between them is variously heroic, anguished, pathetic, feeble and farcical; echoing through it is the refrain "Faustus be resolute," which is painfully impossible amid these varying senses of mankind. When the play turns tragic in its final twist, Faustus' collapse is into simultaneous submission to both his bosses:

> See, see where Christ's blood streams in the firmament!
> One drop would save my soul, half a drop. Ah, my Christ!—
> Rend not my heart for naming of my Christ;
> Yet will I call on him. O, spare me, Lucifer!—   (xix. 146)

Faustus is torn to pieces between Love and Fear: either requires submission and so depends on a failure of resolution. That failure appears variously as comic, tragic or farcical: it is always dramatic.

D. J. Palmer

Tamburlaine's world is controlled by Nature: we see nothing of the direct influence of providence, and consequently Tamburlaine seems marvellously free in the exercise of his will. *Dr. Faustus* deals directly with the will of God, and the hero's attempts to defy it: the story has an explicitly theological frame of reference. Nevertheless the main interest is focussed here too upon the human will. Faustus brings about his own tragedy; to the very end, it is within his power to seek God's mercy, but he chooses damnation and persists in his choice. It is finally a tragedy of despair, as Faustus commits this one sin which puts him beyond God's grace.

From "Elizabethan Tragic Heroes" by D. J. Palmer, in Elizabethan Theatre (Stratford-upon-Avon Studies 9), eds. *John Russell Brown and Bernard Harris (London: Edward Arnold [Publishers] Ltd., 1966), pp. 29–31. Copyright © by Edward Arnold (Publishers) Ltd. 1966. Reprinted by permission of the publisher.*

In a precise theological sense, Faustus' career runs through the whole gamut of sins, from pride to despair. The torments of hell, as Mephistophilis warns him, are not located in one place, and Faustus suffers damnation in the despair of his last speech. There is a dreadful irony pervading the play, which amounts to its controlling method of presentation, and this irony, unlike that in *Tamburlaine,* operates at the verbal level. When Faustus first summons Mephistophilis, it is to discover that his words have no compelling power, that the devil came of his own accord:

> For, when we hear one rack the name of God,
> Abjure the Scriptures and his Saviour Christ,
> We fly, in hope to get his glorious soul.

(I. iii. 49)

Later, when Faustus calls upon Christ, it is Lucifer and Beelzebub who answer him. The invocation of Helen, that superb piece of lyric poetry, is shot through with ironic meanings not intended by Faustus, reminding us that this vision is an evil spirit, an illusion in more than the theatrical sense. The action and words constantly serve to divorce the soaring imaginative visions of Faustus' poetry from the realities of his self-elected situation; his desires inhabit a splendid, open world of infinite possibilities, but his choice commits him to an enclosed, inescapable destiny. The last soliloquy seems to concentrate and epitomise all that the play has already shown; expressed with a powerful urgency which arises from its context, Faustus' desperation is embodied in imagery which both contracts and extends the dimensions of time and space. The acceleration of clock-time, and his almost claustrophobic sense of being trapped in his study, are sensations ironically intensified by the imminence of eternity and infinity. This speech is a form of prayer, or a magic spell to suspend the inevitable pace of time, to open up the furthest recesses of heaven and earth. Even the line from Ovid's love poem, *O lente, lente currite, noctis equi,* assumes in its new context the solemnity of an incantation. But here as before Faustus' words are impotent: they cannot command the elements: they transform nothing. The poetry does create a theatrical illusion; its only power is over the imagination, and its imagery summons the whole universe to witness Faustus' end. Unlike *Tamburlaine,* however, the visionary stage of the hero's imagination cannot contain the whole drama. It is encompassed by a much vaster theatre than man himself can create.

Barabbas and Edward II dwell in a diminished world. Here Marlowe shifted the centre of dramatic interest from the titanic hero and his eloquence to the tensions of intrigue and character conflict. His heroes in these two plays do not rise above their fellow-men, though Marlowe's interest in the egoistic, aggressive nature persists. The character relationships in *The Jew of Malta* and *Edward II* are therefore wholly limited to hatred and conflict. The world is atomised: each man is at odds with his neighbour, friendships are unstable and temporary, and the passions at play are unheroic, though fierce and uncompromising.

Chronology of Important Dates

Marlowe	The Age
1564 Christopher Marlowe born at Canterbury, son of John Marlowe, shoemaker; baptized February 26.	William Shakespeare born at Stratford, son of John Shakespeare, glover; baptized April 26.
1576	The Theater, the first London playhouse, built by James Burbage.
1579 Entered the King's School in Canterbury as holder of a scholarship.	
1580 Entered Corpus Christi College, Cambridge; soon elected to a scholarship.	
1584 Received the B.A. degree; continued to hold his scholarship.	John Lyly's *Campaspe* and *Sappho and Phao* published.
1587 Received the M.A. degree and left Cambridge for London.	*Historia von D. Iohan Fausteñ* published at Frankfurt. The Rose Theater built by Henslowe. Mary, Queen of Scots, executed.
1588	The Spanish Armada defeated. "That Atheist Tamburlan" and "such mad and scoffing poets, that have propheticall spirits as bred of *Merlins* race" referred to by Robert Greene in his *Perimedes the Blacksmith*.

1589	Arrested as participant in a street fight in which William Bradley was killed by Thomas Watson; Watson declared by a jury to have acted in self-defense; Marlowe released.	
1590	*Tamburlaine,* Parts I and II, published.	Spenser's *Faerie Queene,* I–III, and Sidney's *Arcadia* published.
1593	May 20: Marlowe arrested by order of the Privy Council to answer charges. May 31: Stabbed to death at an inn in Deptford by Ingram Frizer, who was finally pardoned after declaration by a jury that he acted in self-defense in a quarrel over the reckoning.	May 12: Thomas Kyd, suspected of treason, arrested and tortured; papers accounted blasphemous, which he later said were Marlowe's, found in his room; written charges of irreligious and treasonous talk on Marlowe's part made by Richard Baines at nearly the same time. Shakespeare's *Venus and Adonis* published.
1594	*Edward II* published.	
1595		Robert Greene's *Friar Bacon and Friar Bungay* and Shakespeare's *Rape of Lucrece* published.
1597		Shakespeare's *Richard II* and *Richard III* published.
1598	*Hero and Leander* published.	
1603		Elizabeth died; James I succeeded.
1604	*Doctor Faustus* published (the "A-text").	
1616	*Doctor Faustus* published (the "B-text").	
1633	*The Jew of Malta* published.	

Notes on the Editor and Contributors

WILLARD FARNHAM, editor of this volume, is Professor of English, Emeritus, University of California at Berkeley. He is the author of *The Medieval Heritage of Elizabethan Tragedy* (1936) and *Shakespeare's Tragic Frontier: The World of His Final Tragedies* (1950), and editor of Shakespeare's *Hamlet* (1957) and Shakespeare's *Troilus and Cressida* (1966).

MURIEL C. BRADBROOK, Professor of English, University of Cambridge, is the author of *Elizabethan Stage Conditions* (1932), *Ibsen, the Norwegian* (1946), *Shakespeare and Elizabethan Poetry* (1951), *The Growth and Structure of Elizabethan Comedy* (1955), and *The Rise of the Common Player* (1962).

NICHOLAS BROOKE is Professor of English, University of East Anglia. He has written *Shakespeare's "King Lear"* (1964), and edited Chapman's *Bussy D'Ambois* (1964).

DOUGLAS COLE is Associate Professor of English at Yale University.

FRANCIS MACDONALD CORNFORD (1879–1943) was the author of many classical studies, including *The Origin of Attic Comedy* (1914), *Greek Religious Thought from Homer to the Age of Alexander* (1923), *Before and After Socrates* (1932), and *Plato's Theory of Knowledge* (1935).

MADELEINE DORAN is Professor of English, University of Wisconsin at Madison. She has written *Henry VI, Parts II and III: Their Relation to the "Contention" and the "True Tragedy"* (1928) and *The Text of "King Lear"* (1931), and has edited Heywood's *If You Know Not Me, You Know Nobody* (1934) and Shakespeare's *A Midsummer Night's Dream* (1959).

ROLAND M. FRYE, Professor of English Literature, University of Pennsylvania, is the author of *God, Man and Satan* (1960), *Perspective on Man: Literature and the Christian Tradition* (1961), and *Shakespeare and Christian Doctrine* (1963).

DAME HELEN GARDNER is Merton Professor of English Literature, University of Oxford. She has written *The Art of T. S. Eliot* (1949), *The Limits of Literary Criticism: Reflections on the Interpretations of Poetry and Scripture* (1956), *The Business of Literary Criticism* (1959), and *Literary Studies* (1967). She has edited *The Metaphysical Poets* (1957), *John Donne: A Collection of Critical Essays* (1962), and *John Donne: The Elegies and the Songs and Sonnets* (1965).

LEO KIRSCHBAUM (1907–1962) taught English (1945–1962) at Wayne State University. He wrote *The True Text of "King Lear"* (1945), *Shakespeare and the Stationers* (1955), *Character and Characterization in Shakespeare* (1962), and edited *Edmund Spenser: Selected Poetry* (1961).

L. C. KNIGHTS, King Edward VII Professor of English Literature, University of Cambridge, is the author of *Drama and Society in the Age of Jonson* (1937), *Explorations: Essays in Criticism Mainly on the Literature of the Seventeenth Century* (1946), *Some Shakespearean Themes* (1959), and *An Approach to Hamlet* (1960).

PAUL H. KOCHER is Professor of English, Stanford University, and the author of *Science and Religion in Elizabethan England* (1953). His edition of *Doctor Faustus* appeared in 1950.

CLIFFORD LEECH is Professor of English, University of Toronto. He is the author of *Shakespeare's Tragedies and Other Studies in Seventeenth Century Drama* (1950), *John Ford and the Drama of His Time* (1957), *The John Fletcher Plays* (1962), *O'Neill* (1963), and *Webster: The Duchess of Malfi* (1963). He is general editor of The Revels Plays and also editor of *Marlowe: A Collection of Critical Essays* (1964).

HARRY LEVIN, Babbit Professor of Comparative Literature, Harvard University, is the author of *James Joyce: A Critical Introduction* (1941), *Contexts of Criticism* (1957), *The Power of Blackness: Hawthorne, Poe, Melville* (1958), *The Question of Hamlet* (1960), *The Gates of Horn: A Study of Five French Realists* (1963), *Refractions: Essays in Comparative Literature* (1966), and editor of *The Portable James Joyce* (1947) and Shakespeare's *Coriolanus* (1956).

D. J. PALMER is Lecturer in English, University of Hull, and the author of *The Rise of English Studies* (1965).

MICHEL POIRIER, Professor of English Literature, the Sorbonne, has written *Sir Philip Sidney: Le Chevalier Poète Elizabethain* (1948).

IRVING RIBNER is Professor of English, University of Delaware. He has written *The English History Play in the Age of Shakespeare* (1957), *Patterns in Shakespearean Tragedy* (1960), *Jacobean Tragedy: The Quest for Moral Order* (1962), and *Tudor and Stuart Drama* (1966). He has edited *The Complete Plays of Marlowe* (1963), Tourneur's *The Atheist's Tragedy* (1964), and *Christopher Marlowe's Dr. Faustus: Text and Major Criticism* (1966).

GEORGE SANTAYANA (1863–1952), a major philosopher and critic, taught philosophy at Harvard University (1889–1911). Among his many works are *The Sense of Beauty* (1896), *The Life of Reason* (1905–1906), *Winds of Doctrine: Studies in Contemporary Opinion* (1912), *Scepticism and Animal Faith* (1923), and *Realms of Being* (1927–1940).

RICHARD B. SEWALL, Professor of English, Yale University, is editor of *Emily Dickinson: A Collection of Critical Essays* (1963), and co-editor, with Laurence Michel, of *Tragedy: Modern Essays in Criticism* (1963).

JAMES SMITH has contributed frequently to *Scrutiny* from the first volume (1932–33) onward. Among his critical essays there published are "On Metaphysical Poetry" (December 1933), "George Chapman" (March and June 1935), and "The Tragedy of Blood" (December 1939).

J. B. STEANE teaches English at the Merchant Taylors' School in England. He is the author of *Tennyson* (1966) and editor of Dekker's *The Shoemaker's Holiday* (1965) and Jonson's *The Alchemist* (1967). His edition of Marlowe's plays is about to be published.

F. P. WILSON (1889–1963) was Merton Professor of English Literature, University of Oxford (1947–1957). He wrote *Elizabethan and Jacobean* (1943) and *Seventeenth Century Prose* (1959), and was general editor (1948–1960) for the Malone Society and co-editor (1945–1963), with Bonamy Dobrée, of *The Oxford History of English Literature.*

Selected Bibliography

*(Supplemental to Notations of Works from
Which Selections Have Been Reprinted)*

Bakeless, John, *The Tragicall History of Christopher Marlowe.* Cambridge, Massachusetts: Harvard University Press, 1942, 2 vols. An informative study, in much detail, of Marlowe's life and works.

Bevington, David M., *From Mankind to Marlowe: Growth of Structure in the Popular Drama of Tudor England.* Cambridge, Massachusetts: Harvard University Press, 1962. A revealing appraisal.

Brockbank, J. P., *Marlowe: Dr. Faustus (Studies in English Literature 6).* London: Edward Arnold, Ltd., 1962. A challenging examination of the play "in both its aspects—Morality and Heroic Tragedy."

Campbell, Lily B., "Doctor Faustus: A Case of Conscience," *Publications of the Modern Language Association,* LXVII (1952), 219–39. Offers parallels between the case of Doctor Faustus and that of the Italian Francis Spira (Francesco Spiera), a recanter of the Protestant faith upon whose agonies of conscience Nathaniel Woodes based an English play, *The Conflict of Conscience* (published 1581).

Eccles, Mark, *Christopher Marlowe in London.* Cambridge, Massachusetts: Harvard University Press, 1934. Adds much to the shaping of Marlowe biography that results from searching of records.

Ellis-Fermor, U. M., *Christopher Marlowe.* London: Methuen & Co., Ltd., 1927. An approach by a critic who, in this and later work, contributes distinctively to the twentieth-century view of Marlowe.

Greg, W. W., "The Damnation of Faustus," *Modern Language Review,* XLI (1946), 97–107. An essay resulting from the author's significant work upon the text of *Doctor Faustus.*

Heilman, Robert B., "The Tragedy of Knowledge: Marlowe's Treatment of Faustus," *Quarterly Review of Literature,* II (1946), 316–32. "Faustus' error was in wanting science to do the work of philosophy and religion."

Hotson, J. Leslie, *The Death of Christopher Marlowe*. London: Nonesuch Press, and Cambridge, Massachusetts: Harvard University Press, 1925. The discovery, through the author's searching of records, of the way Marlowe died.

Mahood, M. M., *Poetry and Humanism*. London: Jonathan Cape, Ltd., 1950. In a perceptive chapter entitled "Marlowe's Heroes" the author maintains that Marlowe in his tragedies shows a "moral insight which enables him to trace the inevitable impoverishment of Renaissance humanism."

TWENTIETH CENTURY
INTERPRETATIONS
MAYNARD MACK, *Series Editor*
Yale University

NOW AVAILABLE
Collections of Critical Essays
ON

THE PLAYBOY OF THE WESTERN WORLD
THE PORTRAIT OF A LADY
A PORTRAIT OF THE ARTIST AS A YOUNG MAN
THE RIME OF THE ANCIENT MARINER
SAMSON AGONISTES
THE SCARLET LETTER
SIR GAWAIN AND THE GREEN KNIGHT
THE SOUND AND THE FURY
THE TEMPEST
TOM JONES
TWELFTH NIGHT
UTOPIA
WALDEN
THE WASTE LAND
WUTHERING HEIGHTS